ACRL monograph number 33

The case
for faculty status
for academic
librarians

Edited by

LEWIS C. BRANSCOMB

Chairman, ad hoc committee on
academic status, university libraries
section, association of college and
research libraries

D1558957

American Library Association

Chicago 1970

*Association of College and
Research Libraries Monographs*

EDITOR
Edward G. Holley
University of Houston

EDITORIAL BOARD
Dale L. Barker
University of Miami (Coral Gables)

Richard D. Johnson
The Claremont Colleges (Honnold Library)

Joe W. Kraus
Illinois State University (Normal)

Kenneth G. Peterson
University of Virginia (Charlottesville)

International Book Number 0-8389-3114-6 (1970)

The Library of Congress card number for the
ACRL Monograph Series is 52-4228

The card number of this title is 75-118198

Printed in the United States of America

Contents

Baker & Taylor

=1
~)

26 Oct 71

41528

Preface

In the late fifties the *ad hoc* Committee on Academic Status was established by the University Libraries Section of the Association of College and Research Libraries. Basically, the purpose of the committee was concern with the status of librarians in academic institutions and this concern has expressed itself primarily in the publication of papers by members of the committee and approved by the committee on various aspects of this subject.

Earlier members on the committee were Robert B. Downs, Archie L. McNeal, Sidney B. Smith, David C. Weber, and Arthur M. McAnally, the first chairman. Membership of the committee at the time of its dismissal in 1969 consisted of Leslie W. Dunlap, Carl W. E. Hintz, William H. Jesse, W. Porter Kellam, Robert H. Muller, and Lewis C. Branscomb, chairman.

Although the primary contribution of the committee lay in the publication of papers, it also attempted to provide, within the limitation of time available, assistance and information to librarians who were actively campaigning on their individual campuses for full academic status including professorial rank and title. It seems safe to state that there are scores and perhaps even hundreds of college and university libraries where the fight was and is being waged for full academic recognition and equality with the teaching faculty.

Eleven of the papers engendered by the committee have been published in *College and Research Libraries* from 1959 to 1968 and with the approval of the committee. At the time of publication the committee invited readers' comments and criticisms of the contents of each paper, but received disappointingly few.

Two other papers included in the present volume are being published for the first time.

After long and thoughtful debate the committee made the decision that it would include here only those papers which helped make the case for faculty status. During the life of the committee not all members have seen eye to eye on all points or agreed fully with the central position of the committee. Beyond that the committee was keenly aware of the fact that some of their academic library colleagues do not believe in professorial status and titles for academic librarians and that a number of head librarians and directors of libraries of leading colleges and universities have not provided full academic status for the professional library staff and are not interested in doing so. The committee concedes the controversial nature of the debate and while it disagrees with this opposing point of view, it respects it.

The *ad hoc* Committee on Academic Status requested that it be discharged upon the publication of this monograph, feeling that its basic responsibility had been fulfilled. However, in view of the very strong interest in the subject by some thousands of academic librarians, it recommended that a new ACRL committee on academic status be established on a permanent basis. Since college as well as university librarians are involved, the new committee will be an ACRL-wide committee rather than a sectional one only. The recommended duties of the new committee are:

1. To collect data and opinions concerning academic status of librarians in colleges and universities
2. To publish the results of studies, surveys, and polls
3. To advise librarians attempting to improve their academic status, achieve faculty rank, etc. or to advise those threatened with loss of status
4. To establish desirable and reasonable norms or standards.

The above duties are suggestive rather than exhaustive. The recommendation of this committee has been approved by the Board of Directors of ACRL and the committee has been appointed.

The chairman wishes to express appreciation to the authors of these papers for their contribution to a timely, challenging and controversial topic. In addition, thanks are due to the members of the committee who have been dedicated and long-suffering over the years required for the gestation of these pieces on faculty status.

Lewis C. Branscomb, *Chairman*
Ad hoc Committee on Academic Status
University Libraries Section
Association of College and Research Libraries

Privileges and obligations of academic status

Arthur M. McAnally

Dr. McAnally is Director of Libraries at the University of Oklahoma. His article appeared earlier in *College and Research Libraries*, March 1963.

During the past twenty-five years, most colleges and the majority of universities have recognized the essentially academic nature of the work of professional librarians by granting them academic or faculty status. This movement towards closer identification of librarians with traditional faculty has required a progressive reorientation of library thought and practices as librarians have tended more and more to apply to themselves the truly academic criteria which the classroom faculty apply to themselves.

The application of faculty standards to librarians has required adaptations and interpretations to fit the special circumstances of librarians. Therefore it has seemed desirable to the Committee on Academic Status to state these principles and interpretations, particularly for the benefit of those academic libraries whose professional staffs only recently have achieved this recognition. The privileges and obligations of academic status fall logically into three categories: general considerations of interest to librarians, library administrators, and university administrators; obligations of library administrators; and the newer duties of librarians. All factors intermingled are described below.

1. *The academic viewpoint.* Professional librarians must accept in principle the standards, customs, and regulations governing the faculty of their institution. These factors, while uniform in principle nationally, may vary in detail at different institutions; the local practices should prevail.

2. *Composition of the staff.* Library staffs should consist of at least two distinct and different groups: first, professional librarians possessing academic status who perform duties of an educational and research character, which require professional training for competent performance; and second, a staff of supporting clerical and other nonprofessional personnel who perform under supervision the more elementary and routine tasks. It is recognized that the proportion in each group will vary with the character, the organization, and, especially, the size of libraries.

3. *Qualifications of professional librarians.* All new appointees should possess appropriate academic qualifications (including advanced professional degrees, plus other degrees for certain positions), intellectual curiosity, and sound personality. It is recognized that in large libraries some specialists such as archivists may need specialized degrees and training.

4. *Professional librarians should be eligible for appointment to the traditional ranks and titles* of instructor, assistant professor, associate professor, and professor.

5. *Recruitment.* In recruiting new librarians, usual academic practices should be followed. If it is customary at the individual institution to hold formal interviews with candidates for appointment to higher ranks, then the library administration should hold similar interviews. To these should be invited both librarians and other academic people who might be interested, such as members of the faculty library committee.

6. *Staff participation in government.* If the classroom faculty at an institution utilize the committee system in conducting certain departmental and college affairs, then the library would be well advised to do likewise. This is not to suggest that all policy decisions should be made by committees, abrogating the authority of the director.

7. *Faculty library committee.* The library as a general educational agency should make use of an advisory faculty committee.

8. *Criteria for considering for salary adjustment, promotions in rank, and granting of tenure.* These criteria vary between college and university, from institution to institution, and in the emphasis given to each. Practices of the individual institution should be followed. The commonly used criteria and library interpretations of each are:

   a. *Success in teaching.* It should be recognized that the librarian's own job is a full-time counseling and teaching responsibility of a special kind. Teaching should be interpreted to mean the kind of teaching, either group or individual, direct or indirect, that a professional librarian does. Success in teaching shall be interpreted to mean successful performance of assigned library duties.

   It should be recognized that much library service to students and faculty is on an informal and individual basis, and also that some library activities, while very important to the development and use of library resources and requiring high levels of academic competence, may not involve direct contacts with students at all.

b. *Research or creative work.* These should be encouraged and rewarded. However, it must be recognized that since librarians usually must work thirty-five or forty hours a week or more to perform their tasks successfully, librarians have less time and energy for research than classroom faculty. Time off for research projects should be allowed if possible. High-level administrative studies should be recognized.

c. *Professional competence and activity.* These are as important to the ongoing quality of library work as for teaching. Time off for attendance at professional meetings and travel allowances should be made available.

d. *University and public service.* Librarians need to be active in these areas. It should be recognized that as relatively new members of the academic team, librarians may not have many opportunities for service on university committees for some years.

e. *Administrative services.* Nearly all librarians have some administrative duties, if no more than supervision of nonprofessional and student assistants. Where the librarian has major administrative duties, this factor becomes important in review for promotion or salary adjustment, and the success of this unit should be the general measure of effectiveness.

9. *Academic rank independent of administrative rank.* Just as for the classroom faculty, promotions in rank or salary should not be conditioned upon advances in, or performance of, administrative duties. Thus a teacher of Greek might advance through the ranks from instructor to full professor without regard to whether or not he ever serves as chairman or head of his department. Similarly, librarians should be advanced when appropriate without regard to the proportion of administrative work performed.

10. *Tenure.* Librarians should be eligible for tenure. The conditions and procedures for granting tenure should be patterned after other faculty practices, with modifications as necessary.

When academic status is first granted to the librarians of an institution, the existence of *de facto* tenure for older members of the library staff should be recognized without a waiting period. However, tenure in such cases should not be automatic.

11. *Academic freedom.* Librarians should have the same privileges of academic freedom as the classroom faculty, and also must accept the corresponding responsibilities. This freedom has special application to library resources. Librarians shall have freedom to choose, and shall protect faculty rights to choose, any materials deemed desirable for their work and shall provide access to all library materials without undue restrictions. In protecting

the freedom to read, librarians should have the safeguards afforded to the classroom faculty.

12. *Sabbatical leaves.* Librarians should be entitled to the privileges of sabbatical leave, if an institutional practice, and should be encouraged to make wider use of the opportunity for growth and renewal that this privilege offers. Chief librarians have special obligations to facilitate this professional activity.

13. *Sanctity of contract.* A contract of employment once offered and accepted must be honored, by both the institution and the individual, for ethical and legal reasons. Librarians should adhere to the library's resignation policies and always give adequate advance notice.

14. *Twelve-month salaries.* When librarians are offered twelve-month appointments, instead of the nine-month appointment usual for the classroom faculty, an equitable adjustment should be made in their salaries.

15. *Classroom teaching.* Librarians should be allowed to teach formal classes in library science, bibliography of a subject, or other areas closely related to their regular duties when this can be done without reducing the effectiveness of their regular library work. Time off must be provided for such teaching proportional to the amount of full-time teaching that the class represents.

16. *Distribution among ranks.* An equitable distribution of librarians among the different academic ranks should be sought. It is noted that the distribution tends to be poor where academic status has been in effect a relatively short time.

17. *Rank of chief librarian.* Since the chief librarian or director heads a major academic unit, he should have the rank of a dean in a university.

APPENDIX I. CRITERIA FOR EVALUATION OF LIBRARIANS

The library faculty shall be evaluated on the basis of truly academic criteria such as are used for the classroom faculty. However, some of these criteria need to be carefully defined in terms of professional librarianship, and the emphasis given to the various factors will vary among different types of work. These criteria, not necessarily in order of importance, are as follows:

Teaching or Research Success

Teaching shall be interpreted to mean the kind of teaching, either group or individual, direct or indirect, a professional librarian does. Examples of teaching activity by librarians: teaching formal classes, lectures to classes, instructing library school students, orientation lectures or tours, guidance (vocational and otherwise), advisory work, aiding students to find and use information, certain reference service, promoting cultural and recreational reading, aiding the faculty in using library resources effectively to supplement, enrich, and improve teaching, instructing in research methods, etc.

The librarian's own job is a full-time teaching responsibility of a special kind; if he teaches formal classes he should receive additional compensation. It is almost impossible for him to take time off from his library duties to compensate for the extra work that classroom teaching entails. It should be noted also that many librarians have a dual responsibility; for keeping up in a subject field, as well as in professional librarianship. This too differs from classroom faculty interests.

In the technical (bibliographical) services, research and organizational abilities become dominant factors. Certain forms of teaching are, however, a recurring and often uncredited part of the total activity in the area. Informational or advisory in nature, and carried on with library and faculty colleagues as well as with students, such teaching is most often referred to as assistance in: (1) exploitation of bibliographies, sources of trade information, identification of elusive or erroneous titles, binding criteria, etc.; (2) effective use of the card catalog, serials record, etc.; (3) interpretation of classification system in use.

Success in the above should be rated on: (1) professional knowledge, *e.g.*, bibliographies, structure of card catalog, etc.; and (2) ability to communicate such knowledge to library users in a manner which will increase the user's comprehension of the scope and limitations of the various sources of information and of appropriate techniques for their effective use.

Research success in technical services is based upon four broad areas of competency: (1) ability to identify or describe adequately the bibliographical units constituting the principal professional activity; (2) subject knowledge of breadth and depth adequate for quick comprehension of content and translation into the notation of the classification schedules; (3) extensive knowledge of appropriate sources for further information, either bibliographical or of subject; and (4) sufficient familiarity with current trends in the various subject fields properly to relate new developments to older materials already classified and to adjust, or supplement, subject headings as desirable or necessary. (This familiarity is dependent on extensive reading in the subject and is sometimes supplemented by contact with research faculty in the subject.)

Success in the above is not immediately apparent. Professional-bibliographical ability is perhaps the obvious; clues as to subject competency may be gained from library and faculty colleague satisfaction in locating needed, or desired, material. Dissatisfaction is voiced more frequently than satisfaction and must be evaluated as either failure in communication or as unsatisfactory performance.

Continuing in technical services, research ability in the sense of scientific attitude and consequent action is of the utmost importance in this area. Operational, or action, research can be carried on by the individual as well as by the department or technical services area as a whole. Rating could be based on (1) knowledge of professional techniques, (2) level of intelligence (skill) in application, (3) efficiency of work organization, and (4) recognition of need for, and testing of, new patterns of work organization, either individual or departmental.

Administrative Success

For certain librarians with considerable administrative responsibility, administrative qualities must weigh more heavily than teaching qualities. Some of the factors in evaluating administrative success are over-all success of the unit, cooperativeness with library and subject field administrators and faculty, efficiency of the library, morale of the staff, fairness, decisiveness, imaginativeness, judgment, self-control, etc. These factors are similar to those which determine the success of the head of a classroom teaching department.

Scholarship and Scholarly Interests

As members of the faculty librarians must be aware of the importance of this traditional measure as an indication of professional competence, freshness, and vigor, and of the contribution that continuing scholarship makes to the individual's work. Such activity might be either in library science or the subject field. However, librarians work thirty-five to forty hours a week, eleven months a year and during most of the holiday vacations, and therefore have less time and energy for such activity than their classroom colleagues.

The following might be considered as measures of scholarly and professional vigor: research of national interest undertaken and published; reports of significant developments, additions, exhibits, experiments, or news written and published; editorship of professional publications; preparation of scholarly exhibits; administrative research (controlled experiment or search of literature) directed toward improving the library's services; bibliographical research for local or other purposes, including preparation of subject reading lists and lists of new publications; visits to other libraries to become familiar with their resources and methods of doing their work—especially when directed toward finding answers to one's own problem areas; taking classes in library school or subject department; attending professional meetings or conferences; etc. This criterion is closely related to professional activity. Note that not all scholarly work is published.

Comparisons between classroom teaching staff and professional library staff under present conditions, as to research and publication, is unrealistic because of differences in free time available. Despite the broad definition of research applicable to the library's special activities, more time for research should be provided.

Library administrators should explore methods of providing more time for research and publication. Various suggestions are: (1) create some research-librarian posts, interchangeable among regular librarians who may wish to follow up problems arising in their work, or perform some pure research studies; (2) provide a reserve or emergency staff who might substitute for a librarian engaged in a research project; (3) provide larger staffs, with each librarian given some free time for such activities; (4) greater use of sabbatical leaves; (5) establish institutional journals, perhaps with primary emphasis on acquisitions; etc.

Whereas colleges often are not interested in research capacity and activity, universities always tend to stress research in appointments and promotions. Research is the only tangible evidence of originality and continuing scholarly interests and has come to be stressed because better measures are lacking.

Professional and Community Interest

Librarians also must be evaluated according to activities in and contributions to the library profession, the university academic community, and the university library. Professional activity also is one measure of professional interest and standing. Factors include: membership in professional and subject field associations; activity in local, state, and national library organizations; participation in university activities; promotion of librarianship in the state or nation; active membership on committees; preparing and delivering papers; and participation in extracurricular activities that further the welfare of the university, library, or community. Taking classes in library school also is a desirable professional act. Membership in social clubs should not be discouraged but usually does not contribute to the advancement of the university or library.

It is noted that lack of adequate travel allowances militates against attendance at and participation in professional meetings in many libraries. This condition should be acknowledged, taken into account, and corrected as rapidly as possible.

Educational Attainment

The library field might well be compared with such fields as art, music, and engineering, where the doctorate, although offered, is frequently not required. Years of professional and subject-field training should be the base, rather than the degree, plus some weight for experience in varied situations. However, it is recognized that the actual degree itself also must be considered, even as in art, music, and engineering.

Since librarians must possess competence both in library science and usually in one or more subject fields as well, continuing education through the taking of formal courses is quite desirable. They should be given special consideration for such purposes, and encouraged by appropriate recognition and reward.

Reading

Since all librarians deal fundamentally with books, or more properly with recorded information, it is essential that they maintain competence in librarianship and in the subject field or fields appropriate to their activity through wide and consistent reading of books, journals, and reviews. This activity is essential to sound performance in both readers' services and technical services activities.

Length of Service at Present Rank

Years of service at present rank should have bearing on promotion, but no more than is true of the teaching faculty. However, there seems to be no reason why librarians cannot become full professors if they meet standards of successful performance, administrative success, contributions to scholarship, educational attainment, and activity in professional, university, and community affairs. This should be true irrespective of whether the library unit in which they work is large or small, or whether the major share of their duties consists of teaching, research, or administration.

It is noted that where faculty status has been in effect a relatively short time, the distribution of librarians among different ranks in many universities tends to be poor. A better distribution among the intermediate and upper ranks should be effected as rapidly as possible. Persons qualified for higher rank already on the staff should be promoted in order of merit and tenure as rapidly as budgetary considerations allow.

Personality

Good personality is essential to successful performance of library tasks, affecting not only successful relations and work with the library's clientele and success in administration but also relations with co-workers and staffs in other departments. Some aspects of personality are covered in preceding paragraphs, but this factor is important enough to justify separate mention. Good personality cannot be defined readily, but is recognized easily.

Outstanding Achievement

Outstanding achievement in any area should be recognized and considered, the same as for the classroom faculty.

APPENDIX II. PROCEDURES FOR EVALUATION OF LIBRARIANS

These criteria for promotion in rank or salary should be used as appropriate to the individual person's duties. Judgment should be by persons in the position to know. For a library assistant, these should include his librarian, the assistant director, the assistant librarian for personnel (if any), and the director. For a departmental librarian, the head of the college or department principally served, or the chairman of the departmental library committee also should be consulted. Other persons may be called upon for advice, but in general the success of the librarian shall be evaluated by his superior officers rather than by his colleagues.

These evaluations should be made annually on a systematic basis, including all qualified professional librarians, at the time of considering the budget for the succeeding year. Each librarian should submit on call a record of activities of himself and his staff; this would have to precede the date of the annual report. As to newly appointed staff members, any suggestions for improvement received in the evaluation process should be passed along to the new appointee by his superior officers.

It should be noted that all evaluation may be conducted informally and that no specific weights can be attached to any of the various criteria. The criteria applicable to that individual should be used in evaluating his work. However, some university administrations require brief formal statements in justification of any change in rank or salary for any individual.

Professional duties in university libraries

Robert B. Downs and Robert F. Delzell

Dr. Downs is Dean of Library Administration and Mr. Delzell is Director of Personnel at the University of Illinois. Their article is a revision of that printed previously in *College and Research Libraries,* January 1965.

It is generally agreed that library staffs should be composed of two categories of workers: (1) professional librarians performing duties of an educational and research nature, requiring professional training for competent performance; and (2) clerical and other nonprofessional or subprofessional personnel who will be responsible for more elementary, routine, and mechanical tasks. Considerable support exists among administrators for a further breakdown, *i.e.,* for three rather than two divisions: professional, subprofessional, and clerical. The rationale is that in large libraries many subprofessionals, who would not require library school preparation, could be employed and trained to achieve satisfactory skill in the performance of a few narrow phases of library work.

The percentage of the staff that ought to be classified as professional or academic and the proportion clerical or nonacademic usually varies with the organization and size of the library. As a general rule, experts in administration believe, not more than one half of a university library staff should belong in the professional category, and a ratio frequently recommended is one-third professional and two-thirds clerical. Otherwise, it is probable that professional personnel will be performing clerical and subprofessional duties.

An investigation by Eugene D. Hart and William J. Griffith of the University of Southern California, based on a list of one hundred duties equally divided between professional and nonprofessional, concluded that "professional librarians are involved to a significant degree in the performance of nonprofessional duties." Several reasons were suggested for such situations.

1. Library administrators and supervisors are often oblivious to the problem and to the true nature of professional library duties.
2. A general disregard commonly exists with respect to the assignment of nonprofessional duties to professional staff members.
3. Due to the general shortage of personnel in libraries a pyramiding effect of duties results, and work assignments are sometimes made to professional and nonprofessional staff members without regard to the nature of these assignments.

For university librarians the matter of definition of duties is of fundamental importance in the achievement and maintenance of academic or faculty status. An essential first step in gaining proper recognition of librarians as members of the academic staff is making a clear distinction and separation between professional and clerical duties in libraries. The most valid objection to the acceptance of librarians into academic circles is that in some libraries there are alleged to be too many routine, nonprofessional jobs carried on by "professional" staff members. The administrator can hardly defend as professional such assignments as checking in current periodicals, charging out books across a loan desk, filing catalog cards, typing orders, reading book shelves, keeping financial records, binding pamphlets, and all the other necessary but obviously subprofessional activities that go on in libraries.

As a corollary, since there are only so many working hours in a day, librarians who are required to spend a substantial portion of their time in performing clerical routines must neglect opportunities to make important and useful contributions of a professional character.

The separation in actual practice of the two types of duties becomes more feasible as the library increases in size. In small colleges it is not unusual to find only one full-time librarian—with no assistance other than part-time student workers—who is therefore compelled to do something of everything, even janitorial services. Any institution which can justify the title of university, however, will operate its library on a higher level.

Any absolute division between academic and nonacademic or between professional and clerical duties may in some instances be impracticable. Unquestionably there are certain tasks, borderline in nature, which can be as well done by the skilled nonprofessional as by the beginning professional. Nevertheless the characteristics of the two are sufficiently dissimilar to permit reasonably clear distinctions to be made. Much basic work has already been done in determining which library duties are professional and which are nonprofessional. The most detailed analysis was issued by a subcommittee of the ALA Board on Personnel Administration, under the title *Descriptive List of Professional and Nonprofessional Duties in Libraries* (1948). Therein library activities are grouped under thirteen headings and professional and nonprofessional duties separated in each category. A few years later the California Library Association's Committee on Library Development, under the chairmanship of Edward A. Wight, made a significant contribution to the field with its report entitled "Separation of Professional and Nonprofessional Work in Public Libraries" (1952), much of which has relevance for other types of libraries.

A comprehensive survey and attempt to define kinds of responsibilities came from England in a small book issued by the Library Association in 1962: *Professional and Nonprofessional Duties in Libraries; a Descriptive List Compiled by a Subcommittee of the Membership Committee of the Library Association.* The English study acknowledges extensive dependence upon the ALA list, but it takes into account later developments in library science as well as practices peculiar to Britain.

A number of other references bearing more or less directly upon the question of professionalism *vs.* nonprofessionalism in libraries are appended.

JOB DESCRIPTIONS

In connection with the present study university libraries in various regions of the country were asked to furnish job analyses or descriptions which might shed further light on the matter of definitions. For the most part, the results were meager; either no job analyses had been done or the descriptions were too brief and general to be of value. Among the institutions which have developed reasonably detailed specifications for the several levels of professional librarians are the University of California, the University of Michigan, and the University of Illinois. The organizational patterns are similar, each stating minimum qualifications as to education, experience, knowledge, and ability for all categories, from beginners with professional training but no experience, to advanced standards set for chief administrators. In general, no staff member is classified as professional without a college degree and a year of graduate study in an accredited library school, or equivalents.

For purposes of illustration and comparison, summaries of descriptive data for these three major university library systems follow:

University of California

Since the University of California libraries achieved academic status in 1962, sections of the University Administrative Manual relating to libraries and librarians have been in process of revision and amendment. Currently these criteria are:

Librarian I: Entry professional level. Performs a variety of professional library work under direction. Service in this class would usually be for two or three years during which time careful supervision would be given in order that incumbents be prepared for more independent responsibility.

Librarian II: Full professional level. Performs difficult professional work with considerable independence, applying knowledge of library methods and often of a specialized subject field. May supervise nonprofessionals and/or serve in a team leader role over other professional librarians. Management and supervision, although they may be exercised, do not require the major portion of time.

Librarian III: Performs complex professional work and assumes responsibility for: *(a)* the administration of a moderately large department, branch, or unit; or *(b)* application of difficult analytical techniques to certain aspects of library operations; oı *(c)* development and/or management of specialized collections involving selection of material, guidance in technical processing, interpretation of the collection, and provision of advanced reference service for users.

Librarian IV: Positions in this class are characterized by substantial independent responsibility and action. Incumbents have over-all responsibility, frequently assignable in only general terms for: *(a)* the administration of a large branch, large department, or a group of departments; or *(b)* application of difficult analytical techniques to a number of aspects of library operations, frequently working in great detail on a major element of activity; application of various technologies, machines, and systems to several aspects of library operations or one broad aspect in great detail; or *(c)* development and/or management of a subject collection, selectively developed, to at least the general research level; a group of subjects selectively developed jointly for an academic program; and exhaustive area, language, or subject collection with responsibility for complex problems in developing the collection.

Librarian V: Positions in this class are characterized by a very high degree of independent responsibility and action. Incumbents have over-all responsibility, usually assignable in very general terms for: *(a)* the administration of a very large and complex department, branch, unit, or group of departments; or *(b)* application of complex analytical techniques to major aspects of library operations and the development of new routines and services, using advanced techniques from business and industry as well as from librarianship; or *(c)* development and/or management of: an extensive collection in a major discipline, group of languages, or large geographical area; an extensive specialized collection involving several subject fields and containing material of primary interest to researchers; an exhaustive collection covering a broad subject or important segment of a subject.

Assistant University Librarian: Positions in this class provide administrative assistance to the university librarian. Incumbents are delegated responsibility for the work of groups of departments and for carrying out or directing work of general management, with authority to act within the limits of established policy. With the university librarian they formulate new plans and policy and seek solutions to problems involving the whole library or major areas of the library.

Associate University Librarian: Positions in this class provide the highest level of direct participation with the university librarian in all aspects of library planning and administration. The incumbent is delegated full responsibility for acting as the university librarian's deputy in his absence, and among a group of assistant university librarians and staff officers, the associate is the senior executive officer and carries line responsibility for all specific tasks assigned to him. The incumbent may also be delegated responsibility for a group of departments.

University of Michigan

At the University of Michigan professional librarians are considered "academic." As in California, there are five classifications or groupings below the top level of library administration. The distinguishing characteristics and typical tasks assigned to personnel of each class are set forth as follows:

Librarian III A: This level constitutes the beginning professional level of librarianship and performance of professional duties. Includes elementary reference, cataloging or classification work, or performance of circulation or order routines requiring application of professional knowledge. Professional work performed is reviewed by supervisor for format, adequacy, compliance with instructions. Circulation and some service functions are performed independently but within a limited scope. Typical of such positions are: performance of elementary reference work with work reviewed upon completion, and covering a well-defined subject matter field; descriptive cataloging of material involving few problems in establishment of entries; adapting printed Library of Congress catalog cards; revising filing performed by clerical workers; subject cataloging, with revision, of material in a limited subject matter field with no deviations from approved guidelines; performance of circulation and order routines involving supervision of clerical workers, with primary responsibility for professional functions. Administrative responsibility is not normally found at this level; performance of professional work in departmental libraries in which there is no final responsibility for library administration. Minimum qualifications: an AB or BS degree or the equivalent, and a graduate degree (fifth-year degree) in library science; in exceptional instances, specialized training and/or experience may be substituted for part or all of the educational requirements.

Librarian III B: This level includes all positions the duties of which involve application of professional knowledge or experience in supervision and/or performance of difficult, responsible tasks. Bulk of duties are performed independently; professional duties are subject to review, however, and supervisor is available for consultation when necessary. Typical of such positions are: supervision of professional duties of average difficulty performed by lower grade professional employees; performance of professional duties of a more difficult, technical nature; beginning level of responsibility for operation of a divisional library and providing of reference services therein and initial responsibility for book selection and acquisition functions; initial responsibility for book selection or processing in a centralized acquisitions organization, where professional decisions are required; performance of circulation or order routines of a supervisory or administrative nature with responsibility for a small group of professional or subprofessional employees. Minimum qualifications; graduate degree (fifth-year degree) in library science. In exceptional instances, specialized training and/or experience may be substituted for part or all of the educational requirements; two years of professional library experience, for part of which graduate study beyond—or other than—the fifth-year library degree may be substituted.

Librarian IV A: This level includes all positions the incumbents of which independently perform professional duties of a very difficult nature; or supervise performance of technical duties of a moderately difficult nature; or perform administrative duties comparable in difficulty to professional duties above in a public service department of the library or divisional library; or serve as acting head of a large department, in the absence of the department head, in addition to carrying out regularly assigned duties at the level of Librarian III B. Typical of such positions are: unrevised descriptive cataloger of difficult material including scientific, serial, and foreign publications; subject cataloger of difficult material; principal administrative assistant to the head of a major department, with a definite assignment of specific administrative duties; supervisor of a divisional library of medium scope and complexity (size and scope of collection and nature of service demands are determinative). Qualifications: graduate degree (fifth-year degree) in library science. In exceptional instances, specialized training and/or experience may be substituted for part or all of the educational requirements; four years of professional library experience for part of which graduate study beyond—or other than—the fifth-year library degree may be substituted; administrative and supervisory experience, where appropriate.

Librarian IV B: This level includes all positions the duties of which are to supervise and/or perform the most difficult professional work; or to serve as assistant head of a large department; or to perform administrative duties as acting head of a large department in addition to regularly assigned difficult technical duties; or to be assigned responsibility for a major divisional library. Incumbent performs work without immediate supervision, with responsibility for program planning, library administration, or acts in an advisory and staff capacity to supervisory and administrative officers. Typical of such positions are: supervisor and coordinator of difficult cataloging or classification; deputy head of a large department who may additionally perform difficult technical or reference duties; supervisor of a divisional library of large scope and complexity (size and scope of collection and nature of service demands are determinative); head of a small department who supervises work of a moderately difficult nature performed by professional and clerical personnel, with responsibility for administrative functions inherent in such a position; independent performance of extremely difficult professional duties requiring specialized knowledge and/or experience. Qualifications: AB or BS degree or the equivalent; graduate degree (fifth-year degree) in library science. In exceptional instances, specialized training and/or experience may be substituted for part or all of the educational requirements; five years of professional library experience for part of which graduate study beyond—or other than—the fifth-year library degree may be substituted; demonstrated administrative and supervisory ability where appropriate; subject specialization where appropriate.

Librarian V: This level includes all positions the duties of which are to supervise the activities of a department, usually through subordinate supervisors; includes responsibility for staffing and assigning duties; recommending establishment or major changes in policy and establishing procedures within well-defined library regulations. Included are positions of a policy-making purpose, which may not involve direct supervision of a department, but whose authority and recommendations are of as responsible and influential a nature as those at the department head level. Also included are the supervisors of major divisional libraries who bear primary responsibility for adapting and developing the collections and services to the advanced research and instructional programs of the units served. Qualifications: AB or BS degree or the equivalent; graduate degree (fifth-year degree) in library science. In exceptional instances, specialized training and/or experience may be substituted for part or all of the educational requirements; five years of professional library experience for part of which graduate study beyond—or other than—the fifth-year library degree may be substituted; demonstrated administrative and supervisory ability where appropriate; subject specialization where appropriate, evidenced by a graduate degree in the subject field or the equivalent in training and/or experience.

University of Illinois

In the University of Illinois library, where the professional staff has had academic status since 1944, the grouping is similar, but by rank. The requirements as to education, experience, and personal qualifications are also closely analogous to those of the California and Michigan systems. The duties by level are described as follows:

Library Assistants (half-time; library science students): Perform routine professional duties in the technical or public service departments of the library under immediate supervision. In the technical departments may be assigned relatively difficult bibliographical problems requiring subject, bibliographic, or language specialization involved in the acquisition and cataloging of library materials. In the public service departments may give reference service to students and faculty, compile bibliographies, give special instruction and assistance in the use of the card catalog and special indexes, and assist in book selection. In some areas may supervise clerks or student assistants.

Librarians with Rank of Instructor: Given more difficult assignments in the acquisition and cataloging of new library materials; may assist in the training and supervision of new professional, clerical, or student assistants; offer formal or informal instruction in the use of the library; assist with interlibrary loans and give reference service involving difficult bibliographical problems which require subject, bibliographic, or language specialization and the use of unusual library sources and a knowledge of the general library resources. May be in charge of smaller departmental libraries or special reading rooms, assuming responsibility for reference work in special subject fields, selection and acquisition of books, periodicals, and other materials; assisting faculty and students in their class work and individual research problems; and training and supervision of their professional, clerical, or student assistants.

Librarians with Rank of Assistant Professor: Under general administrative direction have considerable latitude for the exercise of individual judgment in their positions; may have substantial responsibility in the technical departments or may be in charge of departmental libraries or assistant heads of departments or departmental libraries; may act as consultants or cooperate with nation-wide library agencies on policies of bibliographical sources and form; give lectures or conduct courses in bibliography and reference as part of the curriculum of a university department or the library school; if in charge of college or departmental libraries, they may serve on the college or departmental library committee and attend faculty meetings, and must be familiar with the educational policies and objectives of their college or department and alert to curriculum changes in order to provide necessary library materials; have responsibility for reference or research work in their areas and assist faculty and graduate students with their research problems; through their knowledge of acquisition problems, book markets, publishers, resources of learned societies and scientific institutions and organizations, assist in developing library resources; usually active in national and state library organizations and other educational associations.

Librarians with Rank of Associate Professor or Professor: In this group are the Dean of Library Administration, the Associate Dean of Library Administration, the Directors of Public Services and Technical Departments, the Director of Personnel, the department heads (Acquisition, Catalog, Reference, Serials, Special Languages), and librarians of the large college and departmental libraries. The department heads and departmental librarians have responsibilities comparable to those in the preceding rank. The Director of Personnel is responsible, with the advice and approval of the dean, associate dean and the two directors, for securing all library personnel—professional, clerical, and student—and formulating and administering personnel policies. The dean is responsible to the university administration for the operation of the library and coordinating its services with the educational program of the university. The associate dean is directly responsible to the dean and acts for him in the dean's absence; the associate dean also has primary responsibility for the Public Service departments. The directors, through their department heads, are responsible for the work of their divisions; they advise with the dean and associate dean on problems of general library policies, and the preparation of budgets.

Library Clerk II: Assist in routine circulation and reading room service; give out information as authorized; prepare basic library records; do routine checking of records, catalogs, and trade bibliographies; receive, record, and route new acquisitions; make simple changes or additions in catalog and other records; do library filing; keep statistical records; handle mail and routine correspondence; repair books; prepare materials for binding; assist in book inventory; supervise student assistants.

Library Clerk III: Be responsible for the efficient performance of clerical duties in a division of the library as assigned; assist in circulation and reading room services; give out information as authorized; do searching in library records and bibliographical tools; supervise the recording and routing of the routine types of new acquisitions; do library filing, revise certain types of filing, and make additions or changes in library records; prepare statistical and time records; assist in book inventory; care for and issue supplies; train and direct clerical and student personnel; handle mail and routine correspondence; repair books; prepare materials for binding.

Chief Library Clerk: Under general supervision, is responsible for the efficient clerical operation of a principal administrative library unit, including the performance of clerical library personnel, interpretation of library records to staff and faculty, routine bibliographical checking, keeping statistical records, and performing related duties as assigned.

Library Technical Assistant I: Search library files and other sources; do routine verification of bibliographical references; do non-complex bibliographic checking in the English language; identify, order, and process library materials. Do brief cataloging, catalog with Library of Congress cards, establish and maintain serials records. Perform elementary reference work limited to the answering of requests for factual information available in the more commonly used reference tools, or provide information about library regulations, or direct readers to shelf locations or library materials. Direct the activities of a sub-processing unit in a catalog or acquisitions department (*e.g.,* binding preparation). Exercise a supervisory function over student assistants, make up student work schedules, train students in shelving procedures, maintain physical order and cleanliness in the stacks, schedule and direct shelf-reading program. Assist members of the professional staff with serial inquiries, identification of documents, or searching of secondhand book catalogs or auction records. Responsible for a library unit during evening hours or on weekends. Give limited reference and other library service. Perform related duties as assigned.

A number of additional university libraries have drawn up job descriptions of the nature of those presented from California, Michigan, and Illinois; *e.g.,* Ohio State, Oregon State System of Higher Education, University of Texas, Florida State University, and Washington State University. The three series cited, however, are representative.

A claim frequently made in support of academic or faculty status for professional librarians is that librarians are teachers, formally or informally. A report prepared by the City University of New York Libraries Staff Association analyzed this claim in a document entitled "Librarians Are Teachers." The report concluded, in summary:

> The instruction performed by librarians of the City Colleges is both classroom teaching and extra-classroom teaching. For convenience this activity may be grouped into the following categories: (1) lectures on the use of the library and library research tools, given to students of all levels in visits to classrooms; (2) lecture-demonstrations to particular groups in the library, at the request of colleagues on the faculty; (3) the preparation of teaching aids, supplementary to textbooks—such as annotated reading lists and guides to particular kinds of materials in the library; (4) the preparation of visual aids, supplementary to classroom lecture—such as films, tape recordings and displays; (5) individual conferences with advanced students on their problems with term papers, honors papers, and theses; (6) education of prospective librarians; (7) participation in teaching programs, such as general studies, adult education, in addition to regular professional work.

Professional librarians in other college and university libraries are of course performing similar teaching functions.

The ALA Board on Personnel Administration's *Descriptive List of Professional and Nonprofessional Duties in Libraries,* previously referred to, describes professional and nonprofessional duties under the following main headings:

Administration
Personnel Management
Self-Development of Staff
Public Relations
Selection of Material
Acquisition of Material
Cataloging and Classification
Mechanical Preparation of Material
Registration and Circulation
Reference Work
Assistance to Readers
Physical Upkeep of Material
Care of Shelves and Files

Each category is shown to have both professional and nonprofessional aspects, with the professional perhaps predominating in some and the clerical in others. The list is presumably applicable to all types of libraries, and there is no attempt to separate duties peculiar to a university library, for example, from the activities in public, school, or college libraries. There would be some value, perhaps, in trying to pull out of the general list those to be found only, or mainly, in university libraries and to add items which may have developed more recently or were overlooked by the ALA committee. The differences may not be substantial enough to justify the time and effort involved in developing a more specialized list, however, in view of the fact that professional work in all major types of libraries everywhere exhibits the same general characteristics.

For example, and again for purposes of comparison, the detailed position classification standards developed by the United States Civil Service Commission characterize the recognized grades or classes of professional librarians in federal government service as follows:

Librarian GS-5: These classes include positions of (1) librarians receiving training for positions at higher grade levels; and (2) librarians performing assignments of limited difficulty and responsibility.

Librarian GS-7: These classes include positions the duties of which are to perform work of moderate difficulty or limited scope in general library work, library administration, or a special functional or subject-matter area.

Librarian GS-9: These classes include positions of (1) librarians in charge of libraries having a limited special subject collection; (2) librarians in charge of libraries having a range of functions which may include extension service; (3) librarians in charge of administrative units for special types of services or functions, including the performance of library work that is complex and difficult; and (4) librarians performing complex and difficult work involving acquisitions, cataloging, reference, or other library functions.

Librarian GS-11: These classes include positions of (1) librarians in charge of libraries that are separate administrative units and have a range of services and functions, which may include extension service; (2) librarians in charge of administrative subdivisions of a library where the functions and services are such as to require a substantial amount of work of the GS-9 level of difficulty and complexity; (3) librarians performing broad assignments for staff development and administration within an area of a library system; or (4) librarians performing expert work involving acquisitions, cataloging, reference, or other library function.

Librarian GS-12: These classes include positions of librarians having (1) over-all supervision for an extensive library or group of libraries; (2) responsibility for directing a library program within an area such as an Army or regional area, with responsibility for integrating the program with that of the parent organization, or (3) nonsupervisory assignments of exceptional difficulty and complexity.

Librarian GS-13: These classes include positions having (1) over-all supervision for an extensive library or group of libraries containing general material as well as specialized technical or scientific collections; and (2) responsibility for coordinating an extensive library system containing general material and technical or scientific material.

EDUCATIONAL PREPARATION

In addition to the nature of duties assigned, a major element in the classification of library workers as professional or nonprofessional is educational preparation. This is a cloudy area, seriously in need of established standards. A specification frequently stated for a professional appointment at any level is a graduate degree from an ALA accredited library school, yet there are hundreds of nonaccredited programs of library education in American colleges and universities, graduate and undergraduate. What is the status of their alumni? An increasing number of British and other librarians trained abroad are being appointed to positions in the United States. Where do they fit in the professional hierarchy? If an advanced academic degree is a requirement for a position, how is a PhD in library science equated, say, with a doctor's degree in Germanic languages?

Rather than trying to resolve such issues or questions, specifications often fall back on the ambiguous phrase "or equivalent." Clearly, definitions of what is meant by equivalents are needed, if the term *professional* as applied to librarians is to have any significance. Undoubtedly modern librarianship has become complex, making demands for specialists in a variety of fields for which no one type of educational preparation provides a satisfactory answer. Thus sets of standards should be developed to serve different purposes and to recognize different requirements.

Insofar as the present study is concerned, it must be conceded that there has been little effort to identify explicitly criteria that might be applied to determine whether a given duty is professional or nonprofessional. The determination has been largely in terms of illustrative descriptions of typical positions at the several levels actually in use in three university library systems—California, Illinois, and Michigan—and in the United States Civil Service.

This pragmatic approach has advantages, but a more objective statement would perhaps be of greater usefulness for general application. If we analyze for this purpose the criteria developed by California, Illinois, Michigan, the United States Civil Service Commission, and other organizations concerned with library standards, certain common elements begin to emerge. We find, for example, that a professional position could be defined as one in which mature judgment is required, or in which the incumbent is assigned certain types of administrative authority and responsibility, or is expected to initiate and develop policy, or is expected to possess a thorough acquaintance with the bibliographic apparatus of research libraries, or may need a highly specialized subject or linguistic background, or may be called upon to plan new programs in library technology. These illustrative criteria could be considerably extended to help determine the earmarks of the professional librarian as distinguished from the nonprofessional or subprofessional worker in libraries.

REFERENCES

American Library Association, Board on Personnel Administration. *Descriptive List of Professional and Nonprofessional Duties in Libraries.* Chicago: ALA, 1948. 75p. Mimeo. Arranged under thirteen headings, subdivided by professional and nonprofessional duties.

Appleby, J. W. "Professionalism and Counter Duty," *Assistant Librarian,* LIII (June 1960), 123-24. Recommends that contacts with public be through professional personnel, even "despised counter duty."

Barcus, T. R. "Incidental Duties of the College Librarian," *CRL,* VII (January 1946), 14-23. Deals in particular with the librarian's participation in general college and university affairs and duties to his community and profession.

Downs, R. B. "Academic Status for Librarians—A New Approach," *CRL,* VII (January 1946), 6-9, 26. Includes list of typical professional positions in University of Illinois Library, arranged by academic rank.

Hart, E. D. and Griffith, W. J. "Professional or Clerical?" *Library Journal,* LXXXVI (September 1, 1961), 2758-59. Used one hundred professional and clerical duties selected from ALA List to check actual practices in twenty-one public libraries.

Houlridge, D. L. "Division of Staff: A Canadian Example," *Assistant Librarian,* LVII (October 1958), 201-203. List of duties drawn from Toronto public library practices.

Library Association. *Professional and Nonprofessional Duties in Libraries.* London: The Association, 1962. 77p. Descriptive list, arranged under twelve major headings, each divided by professional and nonprofessional classification.

Lochhead, D. G. "I Am a University Librarian," *Canadian Library Association Bulletin,* XIII (December 1956), 100-105. Description of a "typical" day in the life of a university librarian, showing how his time is spent.

London. Northwestern Polytechnic School of Librarianship. *Professional Work for Professional Librarians.* London: The School, August 1958. 10p. (Occasional Paper, No. 12). Discussion by two British librarians, one of duties in government, the other in public libraries.

McNeal, Archie L. "Ratio of Professional to Clerical Staff," *CRL,* XVII (May 1956), 219-23.

Skilling, B. C. "Restrictive Practices," *Assistant Librarian,* L (December 1957), 222-23. Author urges that professional librarians restrict themselves to professional tasks.

Smith, Eleanor T. "What's in a Name?—the Reference Librarian." *NCLA, Odds and Book Ends,* No. 36 (Fall 1960), 101. Analysis of work of reference librarian in a public library.

U.S. Civil Service Commission, Personnel Classification Division *Librarian Series GS-1410.* Washington, D.C.: Govt. Print. Off., 1957. 35p.

Wight, E. A. "Separation of Professional and Nonprofessional Work in Public Libraries," *California Librarian,* XIV (September-December 1952), 29-32, 54, 107-16. Discusses methods of differentiating between professional and nonprofessional duties.

Wilkinson, John. "A Division of Labor," *Ontario Library Review,* XLI (May 1957), 87-88. General discussion of desirability of separating clerical from professional functions on staff.

Williams, Edwin E. "Who Does What: Unprofessional Personnel Problems," *CRL,* VI (September 1945), 301-10.

Criteria for appointment to and promotion in academic rank

Carl W. E. Hintz

Dr. Hintz is Director, University of Oregon and State System of Higher Education Libraries, Eugene. The article here is reprinted from *College and Research Libraries*, September 1968.

The move to grant academic status to librarians has been the prevailing trend for a number of years and is now generally accepted, although the exact definition of academic status remains uncertain. Regardless of the institutional pattern, however, it is evident that academic status does carry with it certain privileges and obligations.[1] Whenever obligations are involved, criteria must be formulated and applied to determine the degree to which the obligations are met.

This paper is an attempt to determine the criteria and the procedures commonly used for the evaluation of teaching faculty and the extent to which these criteria, or modifications thereof, are applied to librarians. From this basis, it may be possible to draft for consideration a statement of policy and procedure.

In order to gather information, a questionnaire was sent to the seventy-one academic libraries holding membership in the Association of Research Libraries plus a group of twenty-nine institutions, most of which were state universities. Replies were received from eighty-seven. Sixteen respondents indicated that librarians did not have academic status[2] and one that "since practically all aspects of this subject are under intense study . . . with a view to overhauling

[1] Arthur M. McAnally, "Privileges and Obligations of Academic Status," Lewis C. Branscomb, ed., *The Case for Faculty Status for College and University Librarians* (Chicago: A.L.A., 1970), p.1-8.

[2] In these sixteen libraries, however, academic status was held by some librarians in five, ranging from the director only to "approximately 43 per cent holding faculty status in one of the college faculties."

the whole plan, we deem it inadvisable to answer at this time." The material which follows, therefore, is based on replies from seventy institutions.

The pattern used in the questionnaire emerges quite clearly in the analyses of responses which follow, with perhaps one exception. One series of questions concerned procedures for reviewing recommendations for promotion with particular reference to the existence and use of a "personnel committee." Within the context of this series of questions "personnel committee" referred to an institution-wide committee to review all recommendations for promotion regardless of the point of origin, as opposed to the device of internal school or departmental committees.

FACULTY RANK AND TITLE

The largest group of the respondents—twenty-six—reported that librarians held full faculty rank and title. In these institutions the criteria generally used for faculty appointment and promotion ranked as follows:

Success in teaching	25
Research and publication	25
Professional competence and activity	24
Service to the university	23
Creative work (artistic, dramatic, etc.)	21
Public service	17
Advanced degrees	1
Length of service	1
Effectiveness in administrative assignment	1
Evaluation of department members of higher rank	1
No general criteria but determined by department concerned	1
By department concerned in part	3

Twenty-two indicated that these criteria, or others in general use on the campus, were applied to librarians and fourteen that they were applied equally. Specific modifications listed were the following:

Doctorate not required for promotion
Greater stress on professional competence and nature of work performed
Less emphasis on publication

One respondent stated that all criteria were modified because of the nature of continuing assignments throughout a forty-hour week; a second that criteria are not rigidly applied "since the nature of our work and our work schedules preclude any great amount of formal teaching, research, or publication." Another made the cogent comment that since different persons apply criteria, they are not applied equally. This undoubtedly holds true elsewhere on the campus.

Seven of the respondents indicated a separate set of criteria based on the general ones (so much so that some checked both answers) in the nature of "almost the same," "additional distinctive criteria for librarians," "librarian's evaluation," or "greater weight to professional activities than to publication and research."

Practice varies, in that twelve institutions had a campus-wide personnel committee to review all recommendations for promotion and thirteen did not. A more important point is that in twenty-one cases the procedure was the same for librarians and the general faculty. Five followed a different procedure; greater reliance was placed upon the recommendation of the library director and his key administrative personnel.

EQUIVALENT RANK

Thirteen institutions reported patterns of equivalent rank; *i.e.,* a Librarian L-LV or L-V series, corresponding to the customary academic titles of rank, such as instructor to professor.

In these institutions, the criteria generally used for faculty appointment and promotion ranked as follows:

Success in teaching	9
Research and publication	9
Creative work (artistic, dramatic, etc.)	8
Professional competence and activity	8
Service to university	8
Public service	4
Educational attainments	1

In applying these criteria, or others in general use on the campus, eight indicated that they were applied to librarians and four that they were applied equally. Specific modifications listed were the following:

Two master's degrees accepted in lieu of doctorate
Greater emphasis on professional competence and performance
Potential for long-term contribution to the institution

Five respondents indicated a separate set of criteria. In general, these represent adaptations of general faculty criteria by expressing them in library terms.

Five of the institutions in this group reported the existence of a campus-wide personnel committee to review all recommendations for promotion; seven did not. Eight of the thirteen libraries stated that the procedure followed was the same as for general faculty. Of the three which indicated a different procedure, the library administration played a greater part.

ASSIMILATED RANK

Seven institutions reported a pattern of assimilated rank; *i.e.,* library title with the rank of . . . (catalog librarian with the rank of instructor). In these institutions the criteria generally used for faculty appointment and promotion ranked as follows:

Success in teaching	7
Research and publication	7
Professional competence and activity	7
Creative work (artistic, dramatic, etc.)	6
Service to university	7
Public service	4

In applying these criteria, or others in general use on the campus, four indicated that they were applied in full to librarians and three others indicated that they were applied in part. On the question of equality of application, two felt that the criteria were applied equally, two in part, and three responded in the negative. Three of the respondents felt that the criteria applied to librarians were not separate from those in general use on the campus. Three felt that they were sufficiently modified as to make them distinct. Four institutions utilized a campus-wide personnel committee; three did not. Two reported exactly the same procedure for librarians as for general faculty. Three reported mixed procedures and two reported different procedures. In the latter two the decision-making power rested with the library administration.

VARIABLE PATTERNS

The fourth group, comprising twenty-four respondents, reveals an almost bewildering array of patterns under the general umbrella of academic status. Sixteen of the group reported that they held neither full faculty rank and title nor assimilated rank. The remainder provided mixed responses or no response at all on these points. In other words, twenty-four groups of librarians with academic status do not fall into readily definable classification.

The following are some illustrative schemes:

Librarians with formal teaching duties hold faculty rank and title with all others holding assimilated rank

Academic status and full faculty rank and title above instructor

Department heads are also assistant professors of library science. Non-department heads have not been assigned rank of instructor, although this could be done if there seemed any reason

No rank or tenure, but all other benefits, including membership on senate, committees, etc.

No rank or membership on faculty, but faculty benefits apply. Some librarians have been elected to membership in a college or school faculty

Faculty status, but no formal rank. Voting power in faculty meetings and eligibility for election to senate and other offices

No rank, but all privileges and responsibilities, such as serving on senate and committees

All rights of faculty, except title and some committee memberships

Fully academic with review for advancement and appointment by Dean of Faculty. Librarians do not carry title unless they (1) hold a teaching appointment or (2) are "with the rank of...." The librarian holds faculty rank and title; seven associate or assistant librarians are "with the rank of...." In effect, all perquisites except rank, tenure, and sabbaticals

Status has been used to include sabbatical leave, voting in faculty meetings, committee memberships. In short, everything except rank or rank equivalent, which is now being sought.

Among this group, the criteria generally used for faculty appointment and promotion ranked as follows:

Research and publication	15
Professional competence and activity	14
Service to university	12
Success in teaching	11
Public service	7
Creative work (artistic, dramatic, etc.)	6
Academic qualifications	2
No general criteria	6

In applying these criteria, nine indicated that they were applied to librarians and five that they were applied equally. Nine respondents stated that separate criteria were used. Eight of the respondents reported the existence of a campus-wide personnel committee to review all recommendations for promotion. In one instance, the committee restricted its jurisdiction to teaching faculty only. Nine replied that the procedures for the promotion of librarians were the same, or very similar, to those for teaching faculty. Of the eight reporting a different procedure, the principal distinction rests in the greater role of the library administration.

Table 1

Institutional Group	Number of Institutions	Per Cent Faculty Criteria Applied	Per Cent Criteria Applied To Same Degree	Per Cent Same Procedure Followed
Full rank and title	26	84.6	56.8	80.8
Equivalent rank	13	61.5	30.8	61.5
Assimilated rank	7	50.0	50.0	16.7
Variant	24	37.5	20.8	37.5

APPLICATION OF CRITERIA

The general tendency, regardless of the exact pattern for academic status, is to use the commonly accepted criteria for faculty evaluation although with modifications or special interpretations in some instances. Table 1 reveals some striking variations in application of faculty criteria, degree of application, and the evaluative procedures for promotion between the four groups of institutions.

Without attempting to read too much into this statistical exercise, it seems clear that institutions which have accorded full rank and title to librarians are evaluating them in terms of academic criteria to a greater extent than those institutions which follow a different pattern of academic status. This finding is substantiated by the fact that the "variant group," where academic status is poorly defined or not at all, makes by far the worst showing in the application of academic criteria. In some cases, in this group, the criteria are simply expressed in terms of a position classification (description) and suitability of the person for that position.

Since one of the major questions is "Should, how shall, or do, or can librarians meet the same criteria as teaching faculty?" it is pertinent to examine the criteria as they pertain to librarians before any consideration is given to the development of different criteria, or even substantial modification of existing ones. Many librarians are already meeting existing criteria, and there is no reason why more should not be able to do so, providing that their position descriptions called for them to do so, and if their work assignments were adjusted accordingly.

1. *Success in teaching.* This criterion requires special interpretation if it is to apply. Some librarians are engaged in formal classroom teaching, and many more engage in informal teaching through their daily work with students in the library. Additional special examples are library orientation lectures and guest lectures on bibliographic resources in subject areas. A possible substitution here would be performance of specific duties assigned in the library. In view of the lack of emphasis placed on teaching as a criterion for advancement in most universities, this factor should not weigh too heavily against librarians.

2. *Research and publication.* This seems to be the major roadblock, particularly as it looms large in the promotion of teaching faculty. The fact that work schedules make research and writing for publication difficult for librarians is a stark reality. Some librarians find it possible to meet this criterion. Perhaps more would do so if it were clearly understood that it is expected of them. Conceivably, more personal recognition should be given to the bibliographical research performed by librarians in support of the research activities of others and in the development of research collections and to administrative, internal studies and reports.

3. *Professional competence and activity.* Demonstrated by performance on the job, by active participation in professional organizations (not limited necessarily to library associations), by evidence of continued growth, by mastery of bibliography, and by evidence of being an informed person in matters of educational philosophy and administration.

4. *Service to the university.* This may take the form of service on university committees, or working with student groups, such as foreign student organizations, honorary and professional societies, and others.

5. *Creative work (artistic, dramatic).* In addition to the obvious—creative writing, musical composition, painting, sculpture—participation in the performing arts, such as theatrical productions and musical performances, qualifies. The planning and preparation of some library exhibits involves considerable creativity.

6. *Public service.* As evidenced by service to the wider community.

FORMAL CRITERIA

Respondents were asked to describe criteria used for librarians if they were separate and distinct from those used for faculty in general and to send examples of rating forms or other materials used in the promotion process if they could do so conveniently. The fact that most of the respondents failed to do so suggests that formal statements of this nature are either lacking in most institutions or are not readily available in convenient form.

THE NEED FOR POLICY

As pointed out at the beginning of this paper, academic status stands badly in need of definition. It is used to cover many differing circumstances, ranging from full faculty rank and title for librarians at one end of a spectrum to highly structured position-classification situations which are considered academic because appointments fall within the jurisdiction of the Personnel Officer for Academic Affairs (Dean of Faculties, Vice-President for Academic Affairs, etc.).

Clarification on this point could take one of three forms; full faculty rank and title, assimilated rank, or equivalent rank. Of these, the preferred pattern is that of full faculty rank and title as being most conducive to the development of a standard of librarianship which will best serve the educational, research, and scholarly needs of the academic community. This is based on the assumption that the contributions of librarians in academic libraries are so closely allied to those of academicians in all phases that at times they verge on the inseparable. Support for this thesis is found in the fact that the institutions now granting full rank and title to librarians are applying generally accepted academic criteria and procedures successfully, and to a greater extent than those institutions which do not grant such status.

A SUGGESTED POLICY STATEMENT

Librarians should be accorded recognition proportionate to their qualifications, experience, and duties. A librarian should hold a graduate library degree or equivalent from a recognized institution, should participate in professional library organizations, and should perform duties of a professional nature. The determination of degrees to be regarded as terminal or appropriate should be vested with the library faculty, subject to the approval of the president. Proper recognition consists of faculty rank, tenure, and salary, and the procedure for advancement provided for other faculty members should apply to librarians.[3]

Criteria for advancement of professional library personnel include the following:

A. Teaching or instructional effectiveness shall be interpreted to mean the special kind of teaching, either group or individual, direct or indirect, that a librarian does. Such instruction may be judged by:
   1. Qualified student and faculty opinion
   2. Informal opinion of colleagues
   3. Effectiveness in the development and use of library resources for undergraduate, graduate, and research programs
   4. Efficiency in the performance of library technical operations supporting instructional and research programs.

[3]Since this will vary from institution to institution, no attempt is made to suggest a specific procedure here.

B. Research or creative work should be rewarded, recognizing the severe limitations on such activities because of the demands on time and energy. This may be judged by:
  1. Publication of books, articles, reviews, and reports of a scholarly nature
  2. Creative achievement involving musical composition, creative writing, original design, skillful production, and superior artistic performance
  3. Preparation of high-level administrative studies
  4. Mastery of bibliographic resources.
C. Professional competence and activity. This may be judged by:
  1. Active participation in professional associations
  2. Efforts for professional growth through further study
  3. Study for advanced degrees
  4. Knowledgeability in matters of educational philosophy and administration.
D. Service to university, including committee and administrative activity, is judged by:
  1. Service and leadership in the internal affairs of the university beyond the duties of the position held on the faculty
  2. Supervision of library personnel
  3. Demonstrated administrative ability and capacity for administration.
E. Public service includes participation on statewide committees, participation in professional activities in the state and nation, consultation, and community service.

Institutional dynamics of faculty status for librarians

Robert H. Muller

Dr. Muller is Professor, School of Library Science, and Research Consultant to the University Library, University of Michigan.

Being a member of the Committee on Academic Status involves a risk. Those who are not acquainted with the task assigned to the committee will assume that any member is necessarily a true believer in academic status for professional college and university library staff members, or possibly faculty titles, and all that goes with such designations. Actually, however, the members of the committee have not always seen eye to eye on all questions, and there have been some differences of opinion on specific issues. One such issue, for instance, is what criteria to use for promotion in rank in cases where librarians have been given faculty titles. Most of the members of the committee believe that criteria very similiar to those used for the teaching faculty should also be applied to the professional library staff, although "teaching effectiveness" has to be differently defined. Whereas, for instance, this writer's view is that faculty rank should be determined primarily on the basis of responsibility, scope, and difficulty of the job assigned rather than as a reward for past scholarly publishing accomplishments, degrees earned, contributions to community and student relations, etc. Despite such differences of opinion, all of the members of the committee seem to be in agreement that faculty status for professional librarians is a positive factor in building morale, recruiting, and promoting optimal performance.

What is not so clearly spelled out or self-evident is in what ways faculty status may contribute to such good results. The following theoretical discussion is concerned with advantages to the institution stemming from faculty status or titles granted to librarians and with the countervailing forces within the institution.

ADVANTAGES

1. *Professionalization.* One of the most beneficial results of faculty status is that it should tend to make librarians more conscious of the essentially academic nature of librarianship and the intellectual role librarians play in the educational scene and to cause their greater involvement in the educational process. Having faculty status or faculty titles should induce librarians to rid themselves of nonacademic duties to the greatest possible extent and see to it that such duties are assigned to nonacademic personnel. In their daily work they should place emphasis on the judgment element inherent in professional library service, as against the emphasis on the maintenance and operational aspects so typical of bureaucratic institutions. Faculty status should cause librarians to focus on developing bibliographic expertise, subject knowledge, and acquaintance with the content of books, etc. It should motivate librarians to become management oriented in the sense of being concerned about objectives, to watch and determine the extent to which objectives are actually achieved, to be alert to possible innovations that improve services or needed services not hitherto made available. Such efforts are professional and deserve status recognition. Much of the responsibility rests, of course, not with the individual members of a library staff but rather with the director or the management team of a library.

We have no evidence, unfortunately, concerning the extent to which the bestowal of faculty status upon librarians actually does produce a greater degree of truly professional spirit among the staff; we merely make that assumption. It would take fairly sophisticated techniques to determine objectively to what extent faculty status actually makes a difference. Unquestionably, there are libraries that provide good service where the professional librarians do not have faculty status or faculty titles; there are other libraries where the staff does have status and titles but the service is not up to par. There are many other factors involved in producing excellence in service, and it is difficult to isolate any one factor. As in so many other areas of behavior, one may have to make an assumption that may be true but cannot be conclusively proved. The reasoning behind the assumption, however, would be about as follows: Since faculty status is a desirable condition in the eyes of many professional librarians, those professionals who are of superior endowment or skill will tend to move into situations where they are given faculty status. Such a tendency would never be 100 per cent true in fact because there are so many other factors—such as geography, salary, type of work, the immovability of some pension plans, etc.—that determine where a given librarian moves and remains in service. However, all other factors being equal, one can assume that, given a free choice, librarians are likely to prefer a position that gives them faculty status or faculty titles to one that does not. One can further assume that once a librarian finds himself in a position where he has such status and the perquisites that go with it, his morale will be higher and he will be inclined to put his best into his work, *i.e.,* more so than if he did not have such status. He is likely to think more highly of the institution he is associated with and identify himself more closely with it. Although these are unproved and perhaps unprovable assumptions, there seems to be a good deal of plausibility in them.

2. *Production of scholarship.* Another assumption that one might make is that having academic status or an academic title should induce a librarian to measure up to the expectations implied in such a title. With such a title, he may be more likely than without such a title to make a contribution to scholarship, even though such a contribution is not necessarily part of his job requirement. He is more likely to be given access to research funds and to obtain leaves for doing research if he has academic status and an academic title than if such designation is absent. Even if the amount of scholarship produced by librarians may not be overly large or impressive, it will tend to make librarians more at home in the world of scholarship and thus cause them to become better librarians.

3. *Identification with one's institution.* Academic institutions are characterized by bestowing upon the faculty the highest degree of prestige and reserving certain perquisites for the faculty only. Although no one would quarrel with an arrangement under which the instructional staff is regarded as more valuable than the auxiliary staff, it is nevertheless true that those who are not clearly identified as members of the elite group are *de facto* reduced to second-class citizenship and deprived of certain privileges that they feel they should have; hence they will be looked down upon, to some extent, by the members of the faculty involved in classroom teaching. There is a tendency among professors to be somewhat self-impressed and status conscious, anyway; and this situation is further aggravated by the fact that librarians are often viewed as playing the role of handmaidens of scholars rather than creators of scholarship. Their true role as "information scientists" and an essential segment of the instructional staff is often not clearly recognized. If the perquisites of librarians are considerably fewer and less favorable than those of the teaching faculty, librarians are also likely to view themselves as second-class citizens and will, therefore, because of this poor self-image, not be sufficiently motivated toward the best possible performance. There may develop a sense of resentment and envy, which is counter productive to good service and will affect performance in a subtle manner at many points. Faculty status and faculty titles will, at least, tend to give librarians a sense of equality and first-class citizenship and will dispel feelings of disgruntlement about unfair treatment or will not allow such feelings to arise in the first place.

It may, of course, be possible to attain first-class citizenship in an academic community without relying on bestowal of official status or titles, but experience has demonstrated that perquisites are more readily and often automatically attained if faculty status and title for librarians are accepted as a matter of course than if each has to be fought for separately and the head librarian has to be continually on the alert for possibly missing out on certain new privileges that are given to the faculty but not to the library staff. This whole matter of attaining perquisites should not have to require the head librarian's time and attention and should not involve a constant battle. Librarians should have the same pension system as the faculty, vacations comparable to those for faculty employed on a twelve-month basis, sabbaticals, and other fringe benefits to which the faculty is entitled. With such first-class citizenship one can expect librarians to develop a close identification with the institution for which they work and thus more fully promote its objectives, and more fully dedicate themselves to the enhancement of its quality.

4. *Fair compensation.* Where librarians have faculty status, one may expect that there will be a greater degree of equivalence between the compensation received by professorial teachers and professorial librarians. This question was referred to in a study by the California Coordinating Council for Higher Education.[1] It was found, for example, that in 1967-68 the average twelve-month salary of the 345 librarians in state colleges was only 0.81 of the average salary of the faculty employed on a nine-month basis. (This relationship did not apply to head librarians, who tended to receive a higher salary for twelve months than the nine-month average salary of the faculty; at the larger colleges, the median was 1.37 as high as the nine-month faculty salary.) Among 529 librarians employed by the libraries of the universities in the California system, the median twelve-month salary was only 0.71 of the median salary paid to the faculty for nine months; although these librarians are classified as "other academic" employees, they have no faculty status or titles. It was evident that both the college and the university library groups were paid less than the faculty, with a slight edge in favor of the state college group. The report states that "the relationship clearly is not one of equality" with the faculty. The study also questions the claim made by librarians and others that the current trend in college libraries is to grant academic status to librarians, "with rights, benefits, salaries, and working conditions equivalent to those of the faculty."[2] The study found that even where academic rank is given in "comparison institutions," half of the institutions do not apply faculty criteria and procedures to librarians in relation to selection and appointment, retention and tenure, and promotion; however, in the majority of the colleges, the librarians are eligible for sabbatical leaves.

[1] See *Annual Report on Salaries and Other Benefits at the California State Colleges and the University of California, 1968-69* (Publication No. 1031; Sacramento, Calif.; Russell L. Riese, Project Director), sec. 4, p.5, 7-9.

[2] *Ibid.*, p.1.

There is, of course, always a difference between what is and what should be, and the majority practice is not necessarily desirable or acceptable. For instance, in this same California study it was found that when the universities in California compared their libraries with unidentified institutions elsewhere which they considered comparable, academic rank was given to librarians (although eligibility for sabbaticals was more widely provided for) in only two out of eight such "comparison institutions." The study also found that in 1967-68, the average salary paid at these comparison institutions and at the universities in California were unusually close, from which observers should not necessarily draw the conclusion, however, that faculty status cannot significantly affect salaries of librarians, considering that the comparison group contained only two libraries where faculty status had been bestowed upon librarians. The California study fails to comment on whether or not faculty status should be given to librarians, but the omission may be indicative of the general attitude of the project staff toward faculty status for librarians: The finding that twelve of sixteen "comparison" colleges do provide faculty status is used primarily as an occasion for comment on the failure of some of these institutions to apply faculty criteria and procedures to librarians, and the finding that six out of eight comparison universities do not provide academic rank for librarians is used only as an occasion to comment on the fact that librarians are, in some cases, eligible for sabbaticals. One may suspect that the omission reflects an unwritten conclusion drawn from the findings, especially with regard to university libraries, namely, that faculty status is perhaps not necessary nor justifiable unless procedures are applied to the appointment, promotion, and retention of librarians in the same way as to the teaching faculty.

The relationship between librarians' salaries and faculty status for librarians has not been subjected to sufficient study. Experience has brought to light instances in which salary increases would be provided for the faculty group only, and the library staff members would be left out of consideration if they did not have faculty status. The results have been observed with regard to certain fringe benefits that are added from time to time to the benefit package applicable to faculty, such as health care provisions, insurance, faculty housing, educational benefits for one's offspring, etc. In one case known to the writer, eligibility to apply for research funds was denied to the library staff for a while because the staff had no faculty titles or teaching duties.

It has not been shown that average salaries for librarians are always better in institutions where faculty status is granted than in those where faculty status is not held. In fact, cynics have pointed out that there are some institutions that do not give faculty status to librarians but which provide better average salaries than other institutions where librarians have faculty status. The situation is further complicated by the contention that some institutions have no salary scale for the faculty; hence any attempt to compare the two groups would make no sense. To compound matters further, it can be shown that there exist wide variations in the compensation of faculty members, depending upon the subject they teach or the school they belong to. (For instance, professors teaching social work or music or education or journalism might receive a much lower average salary than professors teaching medicine, law, business administration, engineering, or science.) Comparisons are further complicated by the fact that differences in rank among faculty members are based on different considerations from those applicable to rank or grade within the library system.

There is no denying that many of these factors make efforts at comparison exceedingly difficult. There are also those who would argue that each separate field has its own labor market, so to speak, and that no institution is required or justified to pay more for librarians than the market for librarians calls for at any given time, and that there is no reason for offering to librarians salaries that are higher than this competitive market demands simply because a given position exists in an institution where professors, by and large, are paid superior salaries as compared to some other institution. In the light of all these difficulties and objections to comparison, superior wisdom is required to come up with any sensible generalizations or prescriptions. Nevertheless, one opinion that may be justified is that if two institutions differ widely in the average compensation for the respective faculties, the compensation for their respective library staff should reflect a similar difference. In other words, if institution A pays its professors extraordinarily good salaries and neighboring institution B pays its professors rather poor salaries, the librarians at the former institution might be entitled to or expect better compensation than those at the latter institution.

Of course, those who claim that salaries are entirely determined by the labor market will object to this prescription on the ground that no institution should be expected to pay higher salaries than necessary, and salary scales are not determined on the basis of humane considerations or theoretical justice, but strictly on the basis of what is required to attract specific individuals to specific jobs in a competitive situation. It would seem, however, that the whole struggle for faculty status for librarians would be considered pointless if the attainment of faculty status did not achieve a sensible and fair relatedness to faculty salary scales, averages, spreads, or similar measures. If the attainment of status is not reflected in salaries and if, by and large, members of the library staff are placed in an economically deprived class as compared to the faculty, the bestowal of status may be viewed by some as delusory. Status should certainly not be resorted to in place of fair compensation. Library managers have had a difficult time thinking this problem through, partly because they are torn between wishing to be fair to the library staff and operating the library as economically as possible.

The labor-management conflict is latent in all library situations. If a head librarian advocates or recommends improved compensation of his library staff without at the same time arguing that it is done primarily for the purpose of retaining the staff and competing with other institutions for quality personnel, he may find himself condemned as an inadequate or incompetent manager, considering that two thirds to three fourths of a library's budget is usually devoted to salary and wage payments. Of course, the salaries paid to professional members of the staff absorb only about half of this amount and, therefore, perhaps do not loom so large in the total picture. In some deprived[3] institutions, library directors have perhaps not pushed as hard for faculty status as might have been possible because the net result of such a change in status might have been a sharp increase in the funds needed to support the library while, at the same time, it would have been difficult enough to obtain sufficient funds for existing services at prevailing salary levels, and more funds for sorely needed books and new services. What directors of libraries have done in many cases is merely to determine what other institutions are paying and attempt to stay in line. If there should be a nation-wide change in the status and corresponding compensation for librarians to bring their pay closer to that of teaching faculty, many institutions will be affected; but since the library profession has no certification procedure comparable to that applicable to teachers or lawyers and is subject to constant influx from a pool of untrained people who are willing to try their hand at librarianship without going through the established program of library education, the library profession is deprived of a sufficiently effective force in bringing about any substantial rise in salary levels even in the face of a shortage of trained and experienced personnel. A change may come about as a result of trade unionization, but moves along that line have not proved to be successful to date because of the reluctance of professional people to identify themselves with tactics historically associated with blue-collar nonprofessionals.

There are those who are inclined to dismiss the whole knotty question by simply contending that the matter of compensation is irrelevant to the question of status. Especially do library administrators tend to argue that status should be justified only on the basis of the contributions which the library staff can make to the educational objectives of the institution and should not be pursued for the selfish end of enhancing the economic status of the staff. Stress is, therefore, placed upon such matters as service on institutional committees, participation in professional associations, publishing, community service, and all those activities that the faculty is usually rewarded for by way of promotion or salary increments. Librarians are encouraged to do all these commendable things but presumably not for the sake of filthy lucre, but only for the sake of demonstrating to the world that they are truly professional, dedicated to the promotion of books and reading, scholarship, information handling, and the preservation of the embodiments of our intellectual heritage in the form of the printed word. As the role of librarians is more deeply appreciated by an

---

[3] *Deprived* is defined in terms of inadequate means in relation to objectives and, therefore, applies to institutions regardless of absolute size of budget or resources.

increasing circle of people, however, their indispensable function can be expected to be reflected in a modicum of attention to fairness in compensation, and perhaps the only realistic way to find fairness on a given campus would be by comparing salaries of librarians to those of the teaching faculty. The conclusion one would like to draw is that either faculty status improves the economic position of librarians in relation to the faculty or else it does not mean all it should. Although this conclusion is one that some library administrators will disagree with, the rationale seems persuasive.

5. *Tenure.* It is often argued that if faculty status is given to librarians, it should include tenure provisions. There are some who contend that unless faculty status includes tenure, it becomes meaningless. A professor without tenure may have reason to be fearful of expressing his views and of exercising the degree of freedom required in controversial realms of scholarship. Some of those who advocate faculty status for librarians contend that tenure is inapplicable or unimportant to librarians. Inapplicability is based on the principle that any member of a library staff should be removable if he fails to perform his duties properly. The contention that tenure is inappropriate is based on the impression that librarians are not often involved in the defense of controversial points of view and, therefore, do not need the protection that tenure gives the teaching faculty. Viewed from another angle, it is also argued that librarians really need not worry about the question of tenure since in most libraries virtually all members of the library staff tend to continue to remain in their jobs and are almost never removed unless they are demonstrably incompetent to perform their duties or are guilty of moral turpitude. Even in such cases, humane considerations often result not in the removal of the staff member, but rather in his transfer to a less demanding or less exposed position where he can still be reasonably useful to the institution and where he can remain until he either retires or voluntarily resigns.

Management thinking would generally argue against tenure for any administrative position, and many if not most professional positions in libraries increasingly tend to become administrative in the sense that they involve supervision of other people and responsibility for planning and on-going operations. From the point of view of the director of a library, it certainly makes his job more difficult if he has to put up with "permanent fixtures" on his staff over whose possible removal he has no control whatsoever. Tenure for librarians should, therefore, be clearly defined as meaning nothing else but continued employment security within the institution and protection against removal on the ground of unpopular views expressed or unorthodox proposals advanced by the staff member concerned. It should not mean, however, any obligation on the part of the library administration or the institution to continue to keep a given staff member or supervisor in a specific position; it should also not carry the implication of seniority rights when it comes to the filling of vacant positions. In this modified sense, then, tenure for librarians would seem to be defensible. Moreover, it corresponds closely to what libraries have traditionally tended to do and would, therefore, not represent any radical change. It would merely give an official stamp of approval to current practice.

6. *Summary of beneficial results.* The thrust of the argument in this paper so far has been that faculty status for librarians can be assumed to yield beneficial results for the institution in which librarians are employed. It should tend to motivate them toward making their work more strictly professional. It should cause them to involve themselves in scholarship and publication. It should strengthen their identification with the institution in which they are employed. It should result in greater fairness of compensation and thus reduce a source of dissatisfaction. It should, finally, give official sanction to the practice of providing continuing employment and tenure within the limits of good administrative practice.

Evidence to substantiate these contentions has not been supplied in this paper. If studies of the results of faculty status and faculty titles are undertaken by researchers, it is suggested that the procedures adopted take account of the many subtle factors involved which do not yield to simplistic analyses. It is obvious that results are not easily or completely measurable, and if tests are devised to provide objective data, care has to be taken that the effects of faculty status are not viewed as being immediate, and that long-range benefits should be considered more significant than immediate effects.

COUNTERVAILING FORCES

The foregoing analysis suggests that the benefits of bestowal of faculty status on the library staff accruing to the employing institution are substantial. It is, therefore, surprising that there is no unanimity on this question among institutions of higher education and that some distinguished institutions (such as Harvard, Yale, Princeton, Columbia, the University of California, the University of Michigan, and the University of Chicago, to name just a few) have so far not seen fit to grant faculty status or titles to librarians across the board. If the benefits to the institutions are so substantial, why is it that such institutions do not take the steps necessary to derive such benefits for themselves?

There are several answers: (1) The teaching faculty is not likely to be enamored with the prospect of having the titles reserved for them adopted by groups they do not consider part of their own profession; to them, the adoption of professorial titles by other groups looks like a diminution of the professorial status. Even though the library staff usually constitutes less than 10 per cent of the total academic staff of an institution, and in some cases perhaps as little as 5 per cent, the faculty is understandably jealous of its prerogatives and fears that if the title of *professor* were to be adopted by other groups, the net result would be a loss of prestige associated with the title. Those who determine policy at institutions whose teaching faculties are exceptionally renowned or distinguished may feel that they have more to lose than to gain if faculty titles were bestowed on those who do not teach or who have not achieved great accomplishments. In any case, it would be unreasonable to expect the teaching faculty to be wildly enthusiastic about the prospect of having librarians brought in as equal members of the elite to which professors belong. The easiest way for a university administrator to frustrate the effort of a library staff toward achieving faculty status is to refer the whole matter to a faculty committee.

(2) The university administrator has become increasingly aware of groups other than librarians which make similar demands for recognition (non-teaching research personnel, audio-visual experts, campus planners, public relations specialists, architectural staff members, systems analysts, etc.). It is clear that if all these groups were brought in under the faculty heading, the professorial title would, indeed, be substantially changed in meaning, and diluted in the eyes of many. There is also the danger that some accrediting bodies may fail to make a distinction between teaching and non-teaching academic staff and may lower the rating of an institution if the number of PhD's is less as a result of having these other groups, including librarians, brought into the faculty statistical count. (3) Unavoidably, there is also the question of possible added cost. As was pointed out above, professorial titles for librarians may result in a greater equalization of salaries between non-teaching and teaching staff; and from the point of view of the budget, the net result may very well be a substantial increase in salary levels for the non-teaching academic staff. Lack of enthusiasm for such a development is not surprising. Benefits to the institution ensuing from faculty status for librarians would have to be very substantial before an institution is likely to pay for it with hard cash. (4) There are also the purists in any institution who will bring their ingenuity to bear on defining professorial status in such a manner that no non-teaching group could conceivably qualify. They would define a professor not as he is but as he used to be, namely, primarily a charismatic research-oriented classroom teacher, and then conclude that since a librarian does not face a class of students and does little research, he is *prima facie* not entitled to being designated a professor.

Other arguments are presented to oppose faculty status for librarians. One of these is (5) that members of the library staff do not govern themselves the way a faculty governs itself; they are not equal partners in a common enterprise, but are subject to an institutional grouping involving subordination of some to others. Therefore, so it is argued, professorial titles are inapplicable unless librarians can see a way of reconstituting themselves in such a manner as to govern themselves as the faculty does. Obviously, such a transformation can hardly be expected to be readily accepted by the director of a given library as long as he is held responsible for the management of the library or cannot absolve himself of such responsibility. When it comes to appointing new members of the staff, for instance, the director is the one who is held responsible for the decision; he does not fulfill this obligation if he merely relies on an executive committee of his staff to make the decision for him. As soon as a university administration insists on having a library managed in exactly the same way as a faculty department is managed, the director is likely to find himself deprived of authority that he needs to carry on the mission assigned to him as director.

The total of these countervailing forces can be very strong, indeed. No matter how forceful a case is presented for faculty status of librarians in terms of benefits to the institution, no university administration is likely to accept such benefits if it has to pay for them through alienation of the faculty plus added budgetary burdens. Where faculty status is not bestowed upon librarians, either the promised benefits to the institution do not seem to be substantial enough or the cost seems too high. There is obviously only one way in which such an impasse is likely to be broken, and that is through pressure exerted by the group that is intent on acquiring the improved status and the benefits that go with it. No matter how much its members might bend in the direction of presenting the case as one involving benefits primarily to the institution, they will find it hard to counter the argument that their prime motivation is to better themselves. In polite society, this issue is rarely brought to a head in such a sharp confrontation. Yet this conflict may well be the heart of the issue. For tactical reasons, it would be most impolitic for the library group to press its case on the basis of wishing to gain benefits for itself; its case has a better chance of succeeding if it is based on benefits accruing to the institution. Yet any sociologically minded observer is bound to detect the self-interest involved. The truth of the matter is perhaps that it is a mixture of both. As the status of librarians is officially recognized and duly enhanced, benefits accrue not only to the librarians involved but also to the institution.

It is not surprising, therefore, that if a labor-union-oriented group presses its demands for faculty status and faculty titles of librarians, as has recently been done at the University of California at Berkeley, it will base its main arguments on the benefits that the institution will derive from such a move, but through the militancy of its presentation it will at the same time reveal the self-interest involved.[4] If the militancy reaches a point at which institutional services

[4]See, for instance, the "Library Improvement Program, University of California, Berkeley," submitted to the university librarian by Rudolf Lednicky, president of the University Federation of Librarians, Berkeley Campus (AF of T, Local 1795, AFL-CIO, P.O. Box 997, Berkeley, Calif. 94701), on August 12, 1968. Among other things, this statement calls for security of employment after three years, assignment to the various divisions of the library the same proportion of the higher academic (or equivalent) ranks as are assigned to departments of instruction, library time for pertinent independent research, access to grants and research funds, sabbatical leaves, evaluation of library administrative personnel by library staff members, moving expenses and parking privileges equal to those available to the faculty, participation in library management, academic freedom, a grievance procedure that involves a hearing by one's peers. Such demands are called "interim measures," pending the granting to librarians of "full faculty status with ranks appropriate to their backgrounds."

are detrimentally affected, the institution is likely to take the demand more seriously than if the case is presented in a half-hearted or self-effacing manner. In view of the ambivalence of the situation, the outcome is hard to predict. It would be foolish, however, for the library group to be oblivious of the strong countervailing forces and to rest its case entirely on the presumably self-evident benefits to the institution concerned.

Library administrators may find themselves in the difficult situation where they honestly desire to do what will most benefit the library staff so as to create conditions that promote the highest morale and thus the best possible library service while, at the same time, they cannot readily endorse all the demands for recognition and compensation that a trade union of staff members presents and that may not be acceptable to the university administration and the faculty. They wish to achieve close identification with the interests of the professional staff from whose ranks they sprang in many cases, but cannot be oblivious of their managerial and institutional obligation.

Professional staff opportunities for study and research

William H. Jesse and Ann E. Mitchell

Mr. Jesse is Director of Libraries and Miss Mitchell is Assistant Reference Librarian at the University of Tennessee. Their article appeared earlier in *College and Research Libraries,* March 1968.

A rapidly changing age is forcing the professions to attach a new importance to continuing education. Librarians realize that while there may be terminal academic degrees, there never can be an end to the continued learning which alone insures against inflexibility in the face of new problems. In this context it is appropriate to inquire into the opportunities for the professional growth of academic librarians. The necessity for professors to continue to study throughout their teaching careers has always been unquestioned, and there has been a long tradition of research in the academic world. It is generally expected that the faculty member will spend a considerable portion of his working hours in these scholarly pursuits. To what extent do similar opportunities and expectations exist for academic librarians? A corollary question is: What opportunities *should* be provided by the employing institution?

To gain some understanding of current practice and thinking on these matters in a cross section of the leading libraries in this country, a questionnaire was sent in December 1966 to the sixty-four academic libraries then belonging to the Association of Research Libraries and to the libraries of twenty-two selected liberal arts colleges. The colleges included a sample from the Midwest and well-known women's colleges of the East. Fifteen usable questionnaires were returned from the college libraries, and fifty-two of the ARL questionnaires were answered. A letter from one university librarian, declining to fill out the questionnaire, explained that the status and privileges of non-teaching academic personnel were currently undergoing scrutiny in his institution. A college librarian wrote that his failure to complete the questionnaire was because no stated policy for such matters had been formulated. The librarians who did respond to the specific questions often qualified their answers with the statement that decisions were made on an individual basis, leading the investigators to conclude that a formal, announced policy having to do with study and research was the exception.

The purpose of the questionnaire was to survey the opportunities provided to professional librarians who desired to pursue further study or to undertake research projects. The term *professional librarian* was broadened to include those performing a high percentage of professional library duties, regardless of whether they had received a master's degree in library science. The emphasis was upon the freedom of the librarian to follow his own initiative; thus assignments from supervisors were not considered to be within the province of the survey. Although "opportunities" may be considered from various viewpoints, such as grants from outside sources and activities of library schools and associations, this study was concerned only with the opportunities provided by the employing institution. Even the librarian's freedom to take advantage of these outside opportunities is largely contingent upon his employer, as represented by both library director and the university or college administration. In the final analysis "opportunity" must be considered in terms of the amount of time and money available. In other words, is the institution willing to release the librarian from assigned duties for a certain period of time—daily, weekly, annually, or after a period of years—so that he may be free to study and to do research? Although leave of absence without pay may be considered by some librarians to constitute an opportunity, for many others some form of financial compensation is necessary to provide real inducement.

STUDY

There is one means of improving the librarian's education which is almost universal, and that is the policy of permitting him to interrupt his working schedule to enroll in classes at the college or university where he is employed. Thirteen of the fifteen college library administrators and all of the fifty-two university library directors allowed professional librarians to interrupt their working schedules in order to attend classes on campus. In one college library there was no established policy, and in the remaining one of the fifteen college libraries the practice had been permitted in the past, but no one had taken advantage of the opportunity in many years.

An additional indication of the interest of the library administration in promoting further study may be found in a modest concession: the granting of time for class attendance. Twenty-nine of the research libraries did not require employees to work additional hours in order to compensate for the time spent in class. Eleven administrators required that the time lost from work be made up. Twelve other administrators gave qualified answers to the effect that decisions were made on an individual basis, depending upon such factors as whether the course was directly related to the librarian's work or was taken at the request of the library. The college librarians leaned heavily towards making decisions on the basis of particular cases.

A third question dealt with the amount of time which was given to the librarians for the purpose of attending class. Responses from the research libraries were from one-half hour to six hours a week, with three hours being the number most frequently mentioned. Several respondents did not specify the number of hours but indicated that it was permissible for librarians to enroll in one course per term.

It is interesting to note that head librarians are not discriminative in most cases concerning the kind of courses which their staffs elect to take during working hours. Only one of fourteen college librarians and not a single one of the university librarians required the courses to be restricted to library science. Six of the fifty university librarians answering this question required that the classes be on a graduate level, and eleven stipulated that the courses be taken for credit. A further question on specifications was: "Are the courses restricted to those a supervisor thinks are directly relevant to the job?" A surprising two thirds of the university librarians answered "no." Only one of fourteen college librarians replied "yes" to this question, carefully adding his opinion, evidently shared by most of his fellow librarians participating in this survey, that "few courses are not relevant to librarianship in some way."

In one third of the universities participating in the survey, librarians received no reduction in tuition for the courses in which they were registered. Fees were waived in thirteen institutions; in sixteen others there were reductions in varying degrees; and in a few other universities reduced tuition was contingent upon certain circumstances. The situation was somewhat more favorable in the liberal arts colleges, there being no tuition charge in half of them.

When asked to list any special eligibility requirements or restrictions regarding the taking of courses, most of the librarians had no comments. The most frequent statement was that the schedule adjustments must be satisfactory so that normal library operations in the employee's department would not suffer because of his absence.

In an effort to determine the extent to which librarians are availing themselves of existing opportunities, the investigators asked: "How many of your full-time professional staff (excluding those on leave) have taken courses during the past three academic years?" The college library administrators apparently had no difficulty in giving precise data. Thirty-one librarians out of a total of 106, or 29 per cent, had taken courses during the past three years. The number ranged from none in three institutions up to two thirds of the staff in one library. It was much more difficult for the directors of large university staffs to answer this question with exact statistics. Such records were not kept in some institutions, and estimates were furnished in a number of other instances. According to the figures or approximations which were reported by thirty-six of the university librarians, roughly 19 per cent of their staffs had been enrolled in classes at some time during the three-year period. In summary, releasing the librarian from duty so that he may pursue formal academic work at his home institution is a long-standing and popular means of upgrading the education of practicing librarians.

RESEARCH

Though many administrators consider continued study to be within the legitimate activities of the librarian, there is less willingness to give time for independent research projects. In answering this part of the questionnaire, respondents were asked to exclude persons employed specifically as research librarians and to disregard library-assigned research. Of the fifteen libraries in the liberal arts group, only one answered an unconditional "yes" to the question, "Is time given from the work schedule for independent research?" Eight indicated that librarians were not given time for research; one director had no policy; the question had not arisen in still another library; and the remaining four librarians in the college group gave qualified answers.

As might be expected, the universities were somewhat more research-oriented, with fifteen libraries releasing staff members from their work schedules for independent research projects and fifteen others—answering neither "yes" nor "no"—implying that such a possibility exists under appropriate circumstances. Although the universities were more favorably disposed towards research than were the college libraries, there were nevertheless sixteen university directors who did not release their personnel for such endeavors. In five other universities there was no established policy pertaining to research. It is interesting to note that one librarian expressed a willingness to give time for research if anyone should request it. Thus it would seem that apathetic librarians must share the responsibility with reluctant administrators for the limited output of research by academic librarians.

To the inquiry concerning the amount of time alloted for research each week by the university libraries, there was a universal reluctance to designate a certain number of hours. All the directors indicated that the amount of time spent on research depended upon the nature of the investigation. In fact, only one librarian even attempted to give an estimation, reporting that as much as one third to one half of the researcher's working time might be devoted to his project.

The directors were further asked if the research conducted by their staffs had to be related to library operations or problems. From the twenty-five university librarians who answered this question, there were eight negative responses, eight positive answers, and nine qualified responses conveying the idea that some relevance to librarianship was desirable but not necessarily required.

More than half of the university libraries assisted the researcher by providing him with free use of photocopying equipment and by making clerical staff available. The colleges were able to offer clerical assistance less frequently. In almost all libraries free interlibrary loan service was given to staff members: Research by professional librarians was supported in still other ways in a few institutions of higher learning. For example, eleven university library directors pointed out that librarians were eligible to apply for a faculty or university research grant. The possibility of financial assistance from the college was also mentioned by three of the liberal arts group.

The final item in the sequence of questions pertaining to research was: "How many professional librarians on your staff have engaged in research projects during the past three academic years?" As in the analogous question on study, it was difficult for the university directors to give precise figures. Fifteen of them failed to answer the question or reported that there was no record. In five university libraries no one had done research during the past three years. At the other extreme, one librarian estimated that 40 per cent of his staff had been engaged in research projects. According to the figures furnished by all of the university libraries, about 8 per cent of the total personnel had been involved in research in the past three years. The comparable figure for college librarians was 14 per cent, or fifteen of the 106 professional workers in the libraries responding to this question. In view of the noticeable difference evident here between the college and university librarians (8 per cent for university librarians and 14 per cent for college librarians), it should be noted that the rough estimates made by the university librarians were probably more subject to error. With large staffs it is more difficult for university directors to keep informed of the activities of their personnel and to report accurate statistics when records are not available. It should also be observed that the college sample represented in this response was small (106 librarians) compared to the 2,523 university librarians in the thirty-seven libraries which presented usable figures concerning research pursuits. It would be a mistake to infer that interest in research is uniformly present among the college libraries. In fact, there had been no research activity during the three-year period in five of the fourteen libraries. In view of the earlier finding that the college libraries in this sample seldom release staff members for research purposes, the college librarians engaged in research apparently were doing much of their work outside their scheduled library hours. At any rate, it is possible to conclude that there is an active group—a minority, to be sure— of both college and university librarians sharing an interest in research.

SABBATICAL LEAVE

In addition to ascertaining the policies and practices concerning study and research on campus, an attempt was also made in this survey to examine provisions for leaves.[1] Of the fifty-two universities, thirty-nine gave sabbatical

[1]For a large-scale study of leaves and other benefits for faculty (though librarians are not considered separately), see Mark H. Ingraham, *The Outer Fringe* (Madison: University of Wisconsin Press, 1965).

leaves to faculty members, and librarians were eligible in twenty-seven of these. Two additional universities had recently adopted plans for librarians, but these proposals were pending approval. In two others there was no formal policy, but some librarians were given a sabbatical in special instances.

Twelve of the fifteen liberal arts colleges had sabbatical plans for faculty members, and in six of these institutions librarians were also eligible. In two additional colleges, only the head librarians were granted sabbatical leaves.

Well-defined standards were in effect in both colleges and universities stipulating the particular librarians who were eligible. These policies varied to such an extent, however, that it was difficult to categorize them. In eight of the universities all professional librarians were eligible; eleven other institutions defined eligibility in terms of faculty rank; for most of the remainder, the criterion was the position held in the library.

In eighteen of the twenty-nine institutions with sabbatical policies for librarians, leave was related in some way to the seventh year of employment; *i.e.*, it was granted after six or seven years of service. Librarians were eligible for leave after three or four years of service in the seven additional universities specifying the length of employment required.

For the majority of universities granting sabbaticals, the most commonly offered alternative was six months at full pay or a year at half salary. Varying lengths of time, ranging from one quarter to one year, were offered; and the librarian in many cases had an option of whether to take more time and less money or vice versa. Plans and policies in the colleges were similar to those in the universities.

There was a variety of responses to the question, "What specifications, if any, are placed upon the way in which the time must be used?" Twelve university directors specified study and/or research. Other answers included activities promoting professional growth, scholarly pursuits, writing, creative work, travel, appropriate industrial or professional experience, and any project approved by committee or administrator. In two universities the librarian was specifically prohibited from using the time to acquire an advanced degree.

Few differences between the policies on sabbatical leave for the teaching faculty and the professional librarians were indicated. In a few institutions leave for librarians may be in the form of a "summer sabbatical" or a summer off with pay after three years of service.

In order that some idea might be gained of the importance of sabbatical leaves in furthering research and study, a question was included on the number of librarians using sabbaticals for these purposes over the past ten years. As no effort was made to determine how long sabbatical leaves had been in effect in the various institutions or to take account of variations in staff size over the years, it would be useless to attempt to give staff participation in terms of percentages. However, simply reporting the number of librarians involved may be of interest. Seven college librarians had taken sabbatical leaves for study, and four were granted leaves for research during the past ten years. The comparable figures for university libraries were fourteen leaves for study and forty-six for research purposes. In addition to the fourteen librarians taking a sabbatical leave for study, there were an estimated twenty-two who were granted "summer sabbaticals" from one university. For purposes of comparison, the total sample (also comprising institutions not granting sabbaticals) included fifteen college libraries with a total professional staff of 122 and fifty-two large research libraries with more than 3,500 professional librarians. None of the librarians had received sabbatical leaves in some institutions in which such leaves were reported to be granted as a matter of policy. Though one college library director asserted that there was no policy on the question of sabbatical leaves, one of his librarians had in fact received a sabbatical for study during the period covered by the questionnaire, showing a further discrepancy between stated policies and practices. One conclusion which can be drawn from the figures presented is that university librarians used sabbatical leave for research purposes more often than for advanced study, whereas the reverse was true of the college group.

SPECIAL LEAVE FOR STUDY AND RESEARCH

An attempt was made to differentiate sabbatical leaves from leaves which were specifically requested for study and research. This effort was not entirely successful since some of the institutions do not distinguish the two.

Just over half of the college libraries stated that special leaves were granted for study, and one third granted leaves for research purposes. The university libraries were much more inclined to grant special leaves than were the colleges, and there was little difference in their willingness whether the leave was to be used for study or for research. Four out of five of the university libraries replied that special leaves could be obtained for these activities. There were qualifying circumstances, of course. In one instance the librarian must already have a PhD degree to be eligible for a research leave.

Two fifths of the university librarians declined to specify the length of leaves granted, stating that decisions were based entirely on the individual cases. Another two fifths indicated that the amount of time was flexible but that periods of up to one year might be granted. In five universities the length of time was specified, and the range was from two weeks to two years.

There was very little financial assistance available from the colleges for any of these special leaves, although there was an exceptional instance in which the head librarian might be given full salary for a half year or half salary for a full year of study. This is the usual provision for a sabbatical leave and may reflect the lack of a clear demarcation between types of leaves.

The universities offered financial assistance for study and research more often than the colleges, but it was difficult to ascertain any specific number because of the many qualified answers and lack of defined policies. Nevertheless, it appeared that fewer than half paid even a portion of the regular salaries to their librarians on leave. One institution offered a special graduate-study leave allowing up to $2,100 for twelve months. In another university, librarians were eligible for a research grant of up to $1,500; and the possibility of a research grant was mentioned in a few other replies. There was no noticeable difference in the policies for financial support of the leaves regardless of whether they were to be used for study or research.

As in the case of courses taken on their own campuses, library directors were permissive about the kind of classes taken during leave. Of the forty university librarians responding to this series of questions, only one specified that library science must be studied during the leave. Eleven of the forty required that the courses be on a graduate level, and thirteen stipulated that the courses be taken for credit.

Few restrictions were placed upon the research done during leave. A college librarian stated his position thus: "Such needs are handled on an individual basis, in order to assist the individual and protect the institution at the same time." One specification was that such research must be done in pursuit of either a doctorate or a master's degree in a subject field. This comment illustrates the difficulty in making and keeping any neat separation between study and research and also raises the suspicion that in other replies the distinction may have been blurred.

In twelve colleges there were six librarians who had secured a leave for the purpose of study during the past ten years; half of them received pay. Only one librarian from these colleges had secured leave for research (four months with pay).

In one fifth of the university libraries which would provide special leaves, no person had secured a leave for study or research in the last ten years. In almost half the libraries willing to grant leaves, no one had taken a leave to do research. In the forty-one university libraries expressing a willingness to grant such leaves, a total of 148 had been given for purposes of study during the previous ten years. Of this group seventy-eight were partially or fully paid leaves. Like the college librarians, the university librarians used leave much more frequently for study than for research. In the preceding ten-year period, forty-five university librarians in all had received leaves for research, of which thirty-two were paid full or partial salary during leave. These should all be considered minimum figures, as the directors' statistics did not at all times extend back the full ten years.

It will be noted that the practices of the library directors have been somewhat more generous than the ill-defined policies referred to earlier would indicate. Though in more than half of all leaves some financial assistance was granted, research was supported more often than study. This result is also at variance with the earlier finding that there was no noticeable difference in the policies for financial support of leaves for the two purposes.

DISCUSSION OF OPPORTUNITIES

Administrators were asked to comment on the importance of the library's providing opportunities for study in terms of the number of librarians in their institutions who had thereby received master's or doctor's degrees subsequent to their professional appointment. One college librarian replied, "This has not presented itself as a 'problem' at our institution since our librarians come equipped with degrees and do not expect the institution to subsidize further education or research study." An opposite viewpoint expressed was that providing such opportunity is "vital to the upgrading of librarianship."

The prevailing attitude among the university librarians was that encouragement of study is an important and desirable policy. Only three directors asserted specifically that it was not an important factor. Some others, however, pointed out that a master's degree was required before employment and that few librarians tried to secure a PhD. Recognizing that ideal educational standards do not always prevail, a director commented: "Enlightened self-interest and responsibility to our profession dictate a policy as liberal as possible."

The question was asked: "To what extent has your staff availed themselves of opportunities for study and research not undertaken for the purpose of securing a degree?" Approximately a third of the college and university librarians answered in the range of very little or minimal. Almost as many university librarians entered the opposite: many, common, or frequently. Some administrators went on to explain that this was a more common practice than studying for a degree among their staffs. Non-degree studying was held to be important especially to increase foreign language competence and for subject-area familiarization.

Librarians were asked to describe any special provisions or unique features which their institutions have with regard to continuing study and research. Two of the college group and one university director mentioned a "summer sabbatical": one quarter with full pay after three years of service. One of the college librarians commented that the thirty-five-hour week and forty-day vacation provided by his institution would make it easier for a librarian to undertake research or study on his own time. In another college the librarian and associate librarian have every other summer free in addition to the regular sabbatical leave. Among the features mentioned by the university librarians were: a graduate study leave with partial salary, a continuing study leave with generous stipend, all-university research grants available to librarians on the same basis as to the teaching faculty, a work-study program, and a twenty-hour management training course for supervisory personnel.

Directors were requested to describe the attitude of the library administration toward further study and research in terms of: (1) strongly urged, (2) encouraged, (3) not actively encouraged but welcomed, (4) permitted, and (5) discouraged. One half of all the college and university administrators checked "encouraged" for both study and research. The next most popular choice for all categories was "welcomed but not actively encouraged." Study received a few more of the "strongly urged" responses than research in both colleges and universities. A slightly larger percentage of the universities as compared to the colleges checked "strongly urged" for study (20 per cent for the universities, 14 per cent for the colleges) and for research (14 per cent for the universities, 10 per cent for the colleges). Although they checked the scale for study, four of the fourteen college librarians did not indicate attitudes on research. Perhaps the question of independent research had not come up sufficiently so that the librarian had a fixed policy or attitude; thus it may have been considered irrelevant to the local situation. Significantly, only one librarian checked the lowest response, "discouraged" (for study); and he qualified his meaning with "*i.e.*, not assisted."

The scale was not sufficiently discriminative for a few directors who marked two alternatives, one university administrator favoring encouragement to librarians taking language courses but indicating a different response ("welcomed" but not "actively encouraged") for degree programs. Another university director asserted that he would "do all that can be done to get librarians to take additional work." There was in his library, he continued, little interest in research; and he would not encourage the weak librarians, some of whom had shown interest. One administrator appended the warning: "Initiative for independent research must come from the individual librarian." Another director wanted it known that he judged further study and research to be important factors in considering staff members for promotions and increases in salary.

Many fruitful comments were elicited by the following question: "What are the similarities and differences in the opportunities for study and research available to faculty members and librarians of your institution?" The most common response from the liberal arts colleges (in five out of thirteen) was to the effect that sabbatical and other leaves of absence were less generous for librarians. Two administrators noted that grants were more readily available to the faculty. "We would probably have a more difficult time justifying time off for study or research than a teaching member of the institution," wrote one head librarian. Realistic assessments of the financial situation led to other remarks, such as "Our budget does not allow for subsidizing graduate education," and "Our staff is not large enough to do more than the daily duties." Although the majority of directors indicated that more opportunities for study and research were available for faculty members, three of the thirteen liberal arts colleges reported that there was no discrepancy in the provisions for the teaching faculty and librarians.

In analyzing the responses to this question from the research libraries, it became apparent that the single most serious difference between the opportunities available to teaching faculty and professional librarians lay in the amount of time which could be set aside for such pursuits. So striking was this difference that eighteen respondents referred primarily to the lack of available time. One librarian pointedly summarized the situation with the comment, "More free time for the faculty." Eleven mentioned specifically the forty-hour scheduled week for librarians in contrast to the flexible schedules of the faculty. Six others referred to the twelve-month contract contrasted to the nine-month period of employment for many members of the teaching staff. This problem is less acute in the college libraries, only one of that group calling attention to differences in the employment year. In addition to these eighteen responses, there were other comments in which lack of time was viewed as one of the primary issues. Six respondents mentioned unequal sabbatical leave policies; three stated that special leave was not available to librarians as it was to the teaching faculty; and one complained of "no time off for research."

One administrator expressed a greater need for study on the part of librarians, who, unlike most faculty members, do not usually hold doctoral degrees. He elaborated, however, that while a librarian may have the advantage of studying for an advanced degree in a subject field in the institution where he serves, the faculty member usually pursues his academic work in another institution. It is interesting that one administrator felt that librarians enjoyed a security denied to the teaching faculty. As he bluntly expressed it, "Faculty are fired if the advanced degree is not obtained in six years. Librarians are not."

Many respondents made pertinent remarks on research, most of them pointing out that faculty members are expected to engage in research as a part of their normal responsibilities, contrary to expectations for librarians. As one administrator asserted, "The librarian's daily activities do not, as a rule, relate to a research project in the same way as teaching faculty." Further, "Librarians' status, salaries, etc., are not governed by their productivity in research," while faculty members feel "compelled to publish." This situation is viewed as advantageous by some directors but as undesirable by those who feel that librarians should be producing more research.

Obviously, there is a great difference between one administrator advocating more peer group pressure among librarians to do research and another who wants us to escape the publish-or-perish dilemma. Contending that librarians are more akin to the administrative faculty than to the teaching faculty, a respondent pointed out that administrative officers do not, as a rule, have time for much research. A university librarian, deploring the idea that forty hours a week is all that a librarian should be expected to devote to his career, declared, "Librarians can find time to do research if they really want to."

Analyzing the difference in financial opportunities available to the two groups, one librarian noted that most faculty leave was financed by research grants and that similar outside financial support had not been available in the library field. The fact that librarians have received little of the funds disbursed by the universities may be at least partially explained, in his opinion, by the failure to request such support. Then, too, although the staff may be encouraged to develop research proposals worthy of receiving grants, a shortage of staff creates problems in releasing librarians from their usual duties. At least one administrator held that the difference between the librarians and teaching faculty of his institution lay not in eligibility for various privileges but rather in unequal rewards to the librarian, as opposed to the teacher, for scholarly endeavors.

A DESIRABLE POLICY

The final and most significant item contained in the questionnaire was this invitation for a summarizing opinion: "What would be your main recommendations for a desirable library policy with regard to providing opportunities for further study and research on the part of professional librarians?" Thirteen college librarians and forty-four university librarians made some commentary, and their ideas, frequently expressed at some length, form the basis for the discussion which follows. So diverse were the opinions advanced that the task of extracting recurrent themes was difficult. An obvious conclusion is that there is no unanimity among academic librarians as to what constitutes a desirable policy. However, probably a majority of the respondents would agree with the college librarian who, without specifying the practical means of implementing the policy, wrote in general terms: "As professionals, librarians should have the opportunity for further study and research, just as they should have faculty rank. Opportunities should be provided when they can be without the interruption of good library service." The dominant idea of extending privileges to librarians on an equal basis with the teaching faculty was present either explicitly or implicitly in most of the recommendations. As one director clearly put it, "We don't believe in a separate policy for librarians." Acceptance of librarians "as members of the teaching faculty rather than administrative officers of the academic community" was a solution offered. On the other hand, an objection was raised to a blanket granting of professorial titles to librarians. One administrator summed up his position as follows:

> There is a conflict, possibly inevitable, between the spirit of scholarship and the demands of library schedules. The librarian's position resembles that of the administrative officer in an academic department who no longer gets around to doing the research he did when he was only a professor. Library policy needs to seek ways of resolving this conflict, if only partially. On the other hand, libraries should strive to avoid development primarily aimed at identification with the teaching profession. In particular, they should avoid being caught up in the "publish or perish" problem, insofar as one exists.

In earlier responses to various questions, directors had revealed a concern for the continuance of good library service, stating a willingness to grant certain benefits provided they could be given without detriment to library operations. Viewing the situation as one of possible conflict between the best interests of the individual and the library, a director wrote: "A balance has to be struck between the advancement of the individual and the work of the library. Insofar as the two can be made compatible, I believe staff members should be encouraged to do graduate study and carry on research, aided by leaves with pay, travel funds, scholarships, etc." Guarding against the problem of a too permissive policy, another librarian set forth a similar philosophy: "A compromise is needed which will benefit the individual, his institution, and the profession at large." One of the favorable points mentioned by a librarian satisfied with the present arrangement in his institution is the flexibility of a policy which will allow the library to "protect itself against the absence of key people at critical moments."

Some other librarians recognize that their own situation stands in need of improvement. The head of a college library enclosed a document which had been prepared for the consideration of the college administration three years ago in which she advocated that librarians be given a summer with pay after three years of service for "improvement" in the form of course work and similar pursuits. She ended her comment with, "I'm sorry to say nothing came of it." A university library director is presently negotiating for the waiver of tuition for graduate courses and for a part-time study and work program. Another administrator simply wrote, "Our own library policy is now under review."

The responsibility of the individual librarian for his own professional growth was stressed in responses such as this one: "Initiative for any research or study not directly connected with a staff member's work must come from the individual." Important factors upon which administrative decisions might be based are the librarian's motivation, and qualifications fitting him to undertake planned programs of research and study. "React to individual cases" was the succinct advice from one administrator. In the same vein was this comment: "Welcome requests and suggested programs for study and research from *able* staff." Also recognizing the primacy of ability, another director advocated leave for research and writing, adding that this prerogative should be confined to those competent to perform these tasks. Still another director, observing that many librarians do not have the desire for continued formal education and research, advised, "Encourage librarians with interest and ability." In addition to motivation and competency, important considerations named in judging the merits of individual cases were whether the individual could be released from assigned duties and the ultimate benefits accruing to the institution as a result of the study or research.

A complex of problems beginning with low motivation prompted this comment:

> Very few librarians in a given institution are interested in or motivated to attempt advanced study and research; the few who are face serious obstacles. Given low demand from the staff, plus the stringencies of library staffing, library administrators have not pushed very hard for perquisites. Given

generally unreceptive institutional atmospheres, they are severely restricted in any case.

Disclaiming the library's responsibility to the individual librarian for his professional development insofar as education and research are concerned, an administrator asserted:

Ideally, it seems to me, we will have few librarians producing significant research until we can recruit to the profession those who have already committed themselves to the scholarly world. In practice, I suppose, this means subject specialists already holding the PhD. The average young librarian, equipped with a BA and a MLS, does not have the intellectual background, training, or experience to aspire to scholarly research however many "how to do it" articles he may write. No library can give him what formal work in a discipline would: there would be no administrative justification for it. He should be educated before we get him. The exception (and praise be, he is always with us) will find the time to do his research if he really feels it is worth doing.

One librarian called for recognition of the products of high-quality scholarship. But another warned that "libraries should continue to use performance of duties as their criterion for tenure and reassignment—supplemented by truly voluntary activities, if they are undertaken, *e.g.*, research." Here we see again an insistence upon individual initiative, an approach which insures the presence of adequate motivation and guards against unfortunate administrative pressure.

Practical suggestions for improving the librarian's lot were given as well as theoretical considerations or ideal solutions. Various practices itemized in the questionnaire and already in effect in many of the institutions were mentioned. Recommendations for sabbatical and special leaves with at least partial salary or grants for study and/or research were specifically made by approximately a third of the university librarians. A failure to mention leave in this unstructured response should not be construed, of course, to mean that it was considered unimportant. The problem, from one viewpoint, was not ineligibility for the sabbatical leave, but a failure of the librarians who were eligible to take full advantage of it. This administrator advocated that eligible librarians formulate a definite plan for study and research as required by their institutions, apply for the leave, and publish the results of their research. One director would like to see a sabbatical used in visiting other libraries for purposes of comparison with the home library, which had been thoroughly studied previously.

In discussing the importance of providing opportunities for study, two administrators recommended that librarians received especial encouragement in seeking advanced degrees in subject specialties, one specifying that time off with pay should be granted for this purpose. A scholarship for deserving librarians who wish to attend graduate school at other institutions was proposed. It was contended that master's or doctoral programs are preferable to random course-taking. Another director, however, advocating leave with at least half salary for study and research, appended this proviso: "Professional leave should not be granted for work toward an advanced degree."

No great differences were evident between the statements of the college and university librarians on the question of a desirable policy. However, in degree of emphasis the responses from the universities more often indicated some concern about providing research opportunities. A college librarian stated that study opportunities should be made more attractive but contended that research in a small liberal arts college library should not be actively encouraged.

In a broad statement of desirable benefits towards professional development in a large university library, sufficient time for research was advocated, together with necessary supplies, student or clerical help, and institutional assistance in obtaining research grants. To facilitate the latter and to serve as informational liaison, it was suggested that a library committee on study and research be established which would serve as advisor to persons seeking grants and publishing results of research. The committee's responsibilities would include an examination of proposed study and research programs, resulting in recommendations to the director of projects worthy of library support. Obviously, such a committee would more readily fill a need in a large university system than in the small college library.

Various suggestions were aimed at the problem of insufficient time to devote to scholarly pursuits. There were recommendations for longer summer vacations, nine-month contracts, and a maximum work week of thirty-five hours. The impossibility of implementing these ideas with present staffing was recognized in most instances. One administrator thought it desirable to incorporate some time for study and research into the regular work schedule.

Money necessarily loomed large in the thinking of administrators; where the lack of sufficient money was not implied as the underlying difficulty, it was explicitly so identified. This is the way one librarian saw the situation: "To permit further study is one thing; to finance it, another. Outside support is essential, such as fellowships, grants." A sabbatical year for librarians, financed in part by foundation or government funds, was the proposal of another. Citing the considerable number of "near-PhD's" in the profession, he advocated that those who could complete their programs in a year should be regarded as the most eligible group. Others eligible might include successful librarians "who need a free year for 're-tooling,' in which they could pursue matters of interest to them without being tied to the rigidities of degree programs or formal research projects."

Sometimes the administrator, while desiring to promote the professional growth of his staff, recognized the practical limitations placed upon his efforts by inadequate financial resources. The librarian of a small system felt that unless some additional money was forthcoming, he would be unable to do more than to release his staff for limited study at the college. Commenting on the difficulties of releasing members from an already inadequate staff, two directors suggested that funds be made available to provide substitute staff while some librarians were away on study or research leave.

Although another director conceded that it would be desirable to free librarians from their professional and managerial duties for study and research, he saw little likelihood of being able to do so. Commenting on the large proportion of clerical employees in relation to professional librarians, he predicted a much smaller percentage of professional staff available in the future for administrative work. Concluding, he wrote: "The sort of staffing that would make possible a major change in the present situation is precluded by: (1) shortage of personnel; (2) budgets of libraries relative to workload."

Viewing the whole problem from the standpoint of the best use of available money, the director of a research library wrote:

> Unless the salary structure of a library is exceptionally good, any extra money should go towards increasing salaries of the best staff members rather than for research or study. If they really want to do research and if it is really significant, a first-class professional librarian will do it regardless of extra money. First-class librarians are in any case difficult to hire without a good or excellent salary scale.

SUMMARY AND SUGGESTED POLICY

Whether a librarian engages in research or continues his formal education is the result of a complex interaction of many factors. Because the role of the library director is crucial, however, it is gratifying to record that almost all the administrators questioned in this survey characterized themselves as welcoming or encouraging further study and research activities among their professional staffs.

One of the main practical difficulties in implementing this attitude is the relative rigidity of the librarian's schedule, which makes it difficult for him to incorporate study and research into his usual activities. The daily schedule requirements were relaxed in virtually all the libraries surveyed, however, to permit staff members to enroll for course work in their institutions. This is a desirable practice, and the administration should further encourage such study by granting librarians the time and by negotiating for the remission of tuition. As befits the role of academic librarians, the administrators questioned did not want continuing education to be restricted to library science but recognized the relevance and value of broad knowledge acquired in the various disciplines.

Because of the difficulty of setting aside time for sustained study and research during ordinary working hours, a desirable alternate or complementary solution lies in the granting of larger blocks of time in some form of leave. Although librarians continue to lag behind the teaching faculty in eligibility for sabbatical leave, there are many institutions in which librarians have equal opportunities. In such cases eligible librarians should be encouraged to apply for the leave and to use it in one of the acceptable ways, study and research being most prominent among these. A large majority of the university library directors expressed a willingness to grant leaves specifically for study or research purposes, and they were more receptive to research proposals under these circumstances than to incorporating research into the daily schedule. A few libraries which do not have traditional sabbatical leaves for librarians have adopted the practice of granting periodically scheduled summer leaves. This innovation seems particularly suitable for librarians; and where traditional sabbatical leaves are lacking, administrators should consider this alternate plan as a realistic means of providing librarians with the necessary time for further study and research.

Most of the academic library directors questioned are aware of the desirability of encouraging the intellectual development of the librarians in their employ, and to this end are receptive to requests from competent, motivated librarians seeking time and support for formal study or worthwhile research projects. Administrators contend, quite rightly, that the individual librarian must take the initiative. It is important, however, for these directors to communicate the receptive attitudes which they have.

Opportunities and activities of university librarians for full participation in the educational enterprise

W. Porter Kellam and Dale L. Barker

Mr. Kellam is Director of Libraries, University of Georgia, and Dr. Barker is Associate Director, University of Miami Libraries. Their article was printed previously in *College and Research Libraries,* May 1968.

The extent to which librarians have the opportunity (and take advantage of such opportunity when it is available) to participate in professional and community activities has been of concern to librarians for many years. The questionnaire on which this study is based was designed to elicit this information from the larger university and research libraries in the United States and Canada. The questionnaire was sent to the directors of all Association of Research Libraries members and to all other state university libraries. Replies were received from seventy-two librarians, most of whom were heads of ARL libraries.

GENERAL SUMMARY

The questionnaire was divided into ten areas of activity in which librarians might participate as parts of the educational enterprise. The first question in each section explored the attitudes of the respondents—usually the library directors—toward participation of staff members in a particular activity commonly engaged in by teaching faculty. These questions were expressed in language equivalent to asking, "Do you encourage . . ." or "Do you think the library benefits by . . ." the given activity.

The responses showed strong sentiment in favor of all these activities, as follows:

	Per Cent
Writing and publication	100
Campus committee and similar assignments	100
Professional service on local, state, and national basis	100
Consulting work	99
Research	97
Surveys	96
Leaves of absence	92
Participation in non-library professional association work	92
Participation in non-professional local activities	89
Teaching	71

Though the value of the precise figures may be questioned, there is a clear indication that library administrators, at least in public, strongly favor the participation of their staffs in professional university life. Some of the affirmative replies to these questions about attitude, however, may not have been very hearty, as indicated by the reservations and qualifications expressed by some of the respondents in volunteered comments. From the evidence of similar comments, on the other hand, some of the negative responses also appear to have been rather weak.

Other questions explored the extent to which this generally high estimate of the value of library staff activity is transformed into policies of support in time, money, and other resources. Many of the observations made by respondents indicated that this is difficult for some. Besides his own attitude, it appeared, the administrator has to take into account the attitudes of others, the costs in relation to resources, the peculiarities of the local academic environment, and other elements. Though the findings in the various categories of activity differed, it can be roughly generalized that about three fourths of the library administrators who favored the involvement of librarians in university activities appeared able and willing to support such involvement at some level and in most categories. This seems indeed like widespread support. The volunteered comments of the respondents, however, indicated that such assistance is often small, it may be extended very selectively, and in some categories the over-all volume of activity on individual campuses is quite low.

TEACHING

Of all the activities in which their staffs might engage, teaching was by far the least popular with library directors. Even so, the 71 per cent who said they encourage it constituted a very substantial sentiment in favor of it. Two thirds of the respondents reported that librarians are given time from their schedules to do teaching, and a remarkable 89 per cent reported that librarians teach courses in their institutions. Librarians were found to teach library science and bibliography only slightly more than subjects outside the library field.

Several points of a qualifying nature should be made. Though most institutions reported some librarians teaching, the comments volunteered by the respondents indicated that the volume of such teaching on each campus tends to be very low. Only a few people on each staff, apparently, possess both the talents and the desire needed for teaching to take place. It is interesting to note that when conditions for teaching exist, library directors usually permit the staff member to go ahead regardless of the director's own attitude in the matter: 86 per cent of those who encourage teaching reported that they had staff members so engaged, but 78 per cent of those who do *not* encourage it also reported the same activity. As to time off, the comments revealed that university policy, rather than internal library policy, often determines what arrangements are made, or not made, to accomodate teaching. Librarians apparently follow prevailing campus patterns whether that be allowed time, extra compensation, or divided appointments.

RESEARCH

The response was almost unanimously in favor of encouraging librarians to do research. Most library administrators are also willing to support research activity: 76 per cent said they allowed time for research, and 83 per cent said they gave some sort of financial assistance. About 60 per cent answered that the research need not be related to library operations or problems, but even so the number of librarians reported as working on library subjects exceeded the number working on other subjects by a ratio of about two to one. For the libraries reporting the number of staff members who had engaged in research in the last three years, the range was from zero to twenty-five people, with the median falling at four.

Though the number of institutions supporting the research activities of staff members was high, support seemed, from the comments, to be extended cautiously, with an eye to the value of the project, the promise of the individual, and the cost to the library. A frequently expressed sentiment was that while assistance was available, staff members should contribute substantially of their own time. Respondents referred to university and off-campus funding to such an extent that it seems likely that support from sources outside the library is playing a prominent role. The kind of in-house support reported to be given by libraries ran mostly to copying service and other easy-to-give assistance in the same categories suggested in the questionnaire.

WRITING AND PUBLICATION

Every respondent said that librarians should be encouraged to write and publish. About 78 per cent reported that they allow time for staff members to prepare articles, though a few stated that they also expect writers to work on their own time as well. Seven out of eight library administrators give some kind of recognition for writing and publishing. By far the most common action was to take this activity into account in recommending advancement in rank, salary, or tenure. Other recognition comes in the form of publicity, mention in official reports, and general commendation and encouragement.

CONSULTING WORK AND SURVEYS

Even though most library administrators regard consulting and surveying as beneficial, the comments indicated that the actual volume of work, free or paid, is very small; and, either because of lack of demand or because the consultant's or surveyor's employer cannot afford it, the volume is not expected to increase much. About 86 per cent of the libraries were reported to give time off for free consulting; 74 per cent would give the time when the consultant is paid. The corresponding proportions for surveys were 83 per cent and 72 per cent. As with some other activities, the staff member who is not given the time seems often to be allowed to charge his time against vacation or to make up the time.

CAMPUS COMMITTEE, COUNCIL, AND BOARD ASSIGNMENTS

If campus committee work were the chief criterion of librarian identification with the educational enterprise, the conclusion might be reached that librarians have progressed quite far in this direction. All library administrators indicated they were generally in favor of this kind of activity, and 98 per cent reported they had staff members serving on campus bodies.

There seemed to be a variety of attitudes toward actively trying to place librarians on faculty committees. About 74 per cent reported they make an effort, but some of these commented that their efforts are modest and infrequent. Some said or implied that on their campuses it is unnecessary, even unseemly, to seek assignments since they will be made by proper authority automatically.

Respondents were not asked to tell how many librarians on their campus hold committee posts, but enough volunteered this information to give the impression that the number varies considerably. The nature of assignments also varies greatly. In status they range from campus housekeeping chores, such as parking or safety, to high-level advisory responsibility. Some assignments (like teaching media, publications, archives) are in areas of some relation to librarianship, but others are of general academic interest. Some draw on the specializations of subject librarians, a conspicuous example (twelve instances) being committees for various area study programs. An interesting, but perhaps predictable, group of assignments (ten instances) has been to committees on computer centers, administrative data processing, and campus ID cards.

PROFESSIONAL SERVICE ON A LOCAL, STATE, AND NATIONAL BASIS

Library administrators not only believe in professional service in library organizations but also seem to support it as much as possible. All of them said they give time for professional activities and almost 99 per cent said they pay expenses. The greatest problem, as might be guessed, is the inadequacy of travel budgets. When resources are low, various schemes were reported for curtailing costs: fractional refunding, low *per diem* allowance, restriction on the number and length of trips, selectivity in persons permitted to travel, rotation of permission to travel, carpooling, selectivity in allowable purposes for travel, and others. Seventy-eight per cent said they paid some expenses to national meetings for staff not on programs or committees. Several who said this, however, indicated that these people were given a lower priority for funds and might in general receive less support than those who had business at the meetings.

LEAVES OF ABSENCE

Directors of libraries generally (92 per cent) thought it beneficial to grant leaves of absence to librarians to study elsewhere, and many of them had had some opportunity to reap the benefits. Eighty-two per cent reported that librarians are permitted by university regulations to take leaves of absence for periods of time usual for other faculty members. It was clear, however, from the comments that the leave might be given with full pay, with reduced pay, without pay, or with some combination of these according to a formula; no data were gathered on which pattern prevails. Respondents from 43 per cent of the institutions reported that librarians had been given leave for study or foreign assignments within the last three years. The examples given showed that the travel had been world-wide and for a great variety of purposes.

PARTICIPATION IN NONLIBRARY PROFESSIONAL ASSOCIATION WORK

Though library administrators favor (by 92 per cent) staff participation in nonlibrary professional associations, their support for it lagged somewhat behind that for some other categories of activity. Time off is given by 85 per cent of the institutions, but expenses are paid (probably to a very limited extent) by only 47 per cent. The comments suggest that the same budget problems exist in this case as for the library associations, but that participation in these organizations is given a lower priority for funds. The questionnaire asked for examples rather than numbers of staff engaged in nonlibrary professional association activity. The examples, along with comments, however, suggest a rather high level of activity and showed remarkable diversity. The organizations mentioned included AAUP and other educational associations; AHA and other historical societies; a wide variety of subject-specialized associations in the arts, the social sciences, the natural sciences, and technology; and several organizations, such as the National Microfilm Association, connected with, or peripheral to, the library and information fields.

PARTICIPATION IN NONPROFESSIONAL LOCAL ACTIVITIES

Though library directors are less enthusiastic over the civic and other non-professional activities of their staffs than over any of the professional activities except teaching, an overwhelming 89 per cent reported they considered it advantageous to their libraries. Few, however, went further than merely to support this kind of activity. Of those who favored such activity, 39 per cent reported that they neither gave time nor paid expenses for it. Just on giving time, the response was fairly divided: 59 per cent give it—at least to some extent—and 39 per cent do not. Very few directors could justify paying any expenses; 86 per cent of those who say they generally approve of these activities reported they do not pay expenses for them.

COMMENTS

It appears that college and university librarians are given extensive opportunity to participate in the educational enterprise when they have the desire and the capability of doing so. There seems to be an underlying fear, however, that participation in the peripheral activities might detract from the basic service function of the library. It is true that most librarians are required to follow a relatively inflexible schedule which cannot be relaxed to any great extent without causing service to suffer.

Because of the differences in the assignments and responsibilities of librarians and teaching faculty, perhaps librarians should not expect to have the freedom of scheduling that teaching faculty have. The library must accept as its main function responsibility for providing the materials of scholarship and research to students, faculty, and scholars. The library cannot meet this responsibility if its staff is allowed to operate on an unorganized or loosely organized basis as does the classroom faculty.

Perhaps there is not so great a problem as would appear at first glance. Probably librarians as a group should not be expected to engage in most of these activities—for example, research and consultation—to the same extent as the faculty. Most faculty either already have or are studying toward the doctorate. Most librarians do not have the doctorate, comparatively few are working toward it, and most library positions do not require it. Many librarians have neither the interest to do extended research nor should it be expected of them because of the nature of their work. Those who are capable and have the desire to do research seemingly have that opportunity in most libraries. Where this opportunity does not exist, the administration would be wise to provide it.

Even if the librarian cannot follow the schedules of the teaching faculty and engage in certain activities to the same extent as the faculty, the nature of his work draws him close to all the educational and research activities of the educational institution. Also he must possess particular academic qualifications and specialized knowledge which the teaching faculty does not have. These justify giving him faculty rank even though certain accommodations must be made.

Tenure for professional librarians on appointment at colleges and universities

Lewis C. Branscomb

Dr. Branscomb is Director of Libraries and Professor of Library Administration, Ohio State University. The article here is reprinted from *College
and Research Libraries,* July 1965.

Professional librarians are involved in intellectual and other tasks that can be
performed only in an atmosphere of freedom. Examples of such tasks are:
(1) the selection of publications, including determination of what to discard
from an existing collection and what to accept or reject from donors; (2) the
determination of restrictions of circulation or access with regard to controversial
library materials; (3) the determination of the degree of prominence in the
shelving of selected library materials; (4) the determination of exhibit programs
involving controversial subjects; (5) the employment of staff members alleged to
have or who express nonconformist opinions, habits, manners, or appearance;
(6) the issuing of bibliographies that might include controversial publications;
(7) the planning or design of well thought out but possibly unorthodox library
facilities; (8) the defense of library policies in the face of unjust accusations;
(9) publishing of articles or books and delivery of speeches in defense of the
principles of free speech and the unhampered pursuit of truth, etc.; (10) the use
of defensible, but unorthodox classifications, subject designations in catalogs,
or labels for books; (11) the adoption of promising but untried methods of
operation or management; and (12) the advising of students as to what to read
or study.

Freedom in the performance of such tasks means the absence of fear of
dismissal or reprisal in the event that the performance happens to arouse the
displeasure or disapproval of governing authorities, pressure groups, or other
self-appointed guardians over mass communications.

Permanent or continuous tenure for professional librarians at colleges and universities is essential for the free and untrammelled performance of such tasks just as freedom is essential for the faculty involved in classroom teaching or research. It implies freedom to carry on the work of the library, conduct research, and engage in extramural activities. It also implies a sufficient degree of job security to make the profession attractive to men and women of ability. Without these indispensable conditions, the professional staff of a library cannot fulfill its obligations to its institution and to society. The privileges of tenure are obvious, but there are obligations which must accompany tenure such as speaking and writing with accuracy, the exercise of appropriate restraint, respect for the opinions of others, and an indication that the librarian is not an institutional spokesman when speaking as a citizen.

The terms and conditions of every appointment should be stated in writing and be in the hands of the institution and of the librarian in advance of the execution of the appointment.

THE ACHIEVEMENT OF TENURE

An institution in which librarians have been accorded faculty rank and title ranging from instructor through full professor on an equal basis with the classroom faculty will appropriately include the professional librarians under the same provisions for achieving tenure as other members of the faculty. This usually involves a period of probation ranging from three years to seven years at the level of instructor or assistant professor, and somewhat shorter periods for the top ranks, with periodic evaluations of the performance of a given faculty member. Professional librarians achieve tenure as to professorial rank, but not as to administrative position or individual assignment.

During the period of probation the decision may be made in any year that the library staff member's contract will not be renewed. Notice of nonreappointment, or of intention not to recommend reappointment to the governing board, should be given in writing in accordance with the following standards:

1. Not later than March 1 of the first academic year of service, if the appointment expires at the end of that year; or, if a one-year appointment terminates during an academic year, at least three months in advance of its termination.
2. Not later than December 15 of the second academic-year of service, if the appointment expires at the end of that year; or, if an initial two-year appointment terminates during the academic year, at least six months in advance of its termination.
3. At least twelve months before the expiration of an appointment after two or more years in the institution.

The staff member has an equal responsibility to fulfill his contract and to provide his institution with a written notice of intent to resign on the same time schedule as that followed by the institution. If the decision is made not to grant tenure, the staff member is so notified at least a year before the end of the probationary period; if appropriate, the library may assist him to find another position for which he is better qualified. It is assumed automatically that a person has achieved tenure at the end of the trial period if he has not been officially notified in writing that his contract will not be renewed. During the probationary period librarians have the same academic freedom that all other members of the library staff and of the classroom faculty enjoy.

TERMINATION FOR CAUSE

Upon the achievement of tenure, the librarian leaves the employ of the institution only through voluntary resignation, retirement, death, or dismissal for cause. Dismissal for cause may be based upon incompetence, moral turpitude, or grave misconduct inimical to the best interest of the institution. In all cases where the facts are in dispute, charges in writing are presented to the library staff member, and the matter is considered by a committee of his peers. Anyone against whom charges have been made is given due notice, is presented with the written charges, and is allowed a reasonable opportunity to reply. The rights of representation, submission of evidence, and the introduction of witnesses shall be granted to both the institution and the person charged, and a full record of the hearings shall be kept. The committee shall make findings of fact, and such recommendations as it may deem appropriate shall be submitted to the president of the institution. A professional librarian on continuous appointment who is dismissed for reasons not involving moral turpitude shall receive his salary for at least a year from the date of notification of dismissal. Termination of a continuous appointment because of financial exigency should be demonstrably *bona fide.* The administrative officer's right to dismiss a staff member for a particular cause may be lost if he fails to inform his staff member of the unsatisfactory nature of his services and does not take the prescribed action within a reasonable time.

While the above statements are recommended for adoption by library administrations where professional librarians are accorded faculty rank and title, in institutions where librarians are under another system, the library administration is advised to establish a tenure procedure similar in nature and principle to that described above. The foregoing statements represent an effort to formalize the best current practice, rather than a marked departure from present practice.

The place of "professional-specialists" on the university library staff

David C. Weber

Mr. Weber is Associate Director of Libraries, Stanford University. His article is slightly revised from that originally published under the same title in *College and Research Libraries,* September 1965.

Within many university libraries there are developing sizable groups which may be termed "professional-specialists." This group of individuals seems to be set apart from traditional librarians by shades of difference in their personnel status within the university and within its library. These shadowy variations are the topic of this paper. A description of the professional-specialist group can be attempted. It cannot however be a precise definition since universities provide great variance in treatment of similar positions, assignments may be combined into hybrid positions, and personnel policies vary widely.

Specialist is here used to refer to an individual with a subject or technical expertise combined with a knowledge of libraries and educational institutions. Although most librarians may be said to specialize (for example, in law libraries or in cataloging of social science materials), the term is further limited to persons whose specialist talents may be said to dominate his talents as a librarian. Using this definition, there would be throughout the country a rather large number of these positions filled with persons having pursued advanced work in the specialty, while there would be fewer with advanced training in both the specialty and in librarianship.[1]

An indication of the dominating interest in the specialty would be the individual's membership and activity in such associations as the Society of

---

[1] There is relevant discussion in Robert B. Downs, "Preparation of Specialists for University Libraries," *Special Libraries,* XXXVII (September 1946), 209-13.

American Archivists, the National Microfilm Association, the American Society for Information Sciences, or the Modern Language Association, and perhaps little interest in the American Library Association, the Law Library Association, or the Special Libraries Association.[2]

Before considering various other ways of arriving at a definition of a distinctive group of positions, the form of the professional-specialist group may be suggested by the following list which is not exhaustive and will surely in the future include new types:

Administrative or systems analyst
Archivist
Area or subject bibliographer
Audio-visual specialist
Book selection specialist or area curator for a language, subject, or region
Building projects manager or facilities planner
Business or financial officer
Editor of publications
Information scientist or data processing specialist
Manuscripts curator
Paleographer
Personnel manager
Photographic specialist
Programmer, computer

Since some of the specialties, such as work with manuscripts, have been a traditional part of librarianship for centuries, it is clear that any list such as the one above is debatable; and a group of professional-specialists can be described and discussed only in broad generalities subject to all the usual hazards of such treatment.

The term *professional-specialists* is not in general intended to designate librarians with assignments in traditional departments who have become specialized due to the unavoidable division of labor which comes with the increasing size and complexity of the library. The amount of "traditional" librarianship which each specialist practices, and which each must know, is so variable that this characteristic cannot be used to help define the group.

Taking another approach, there is likely to be a higher incidence of teaching among the professional-specialists than among the traditionally oriented librarians. Courses of instruction offered by librarians who are subject specialists are common in American universities, as in those abroad. Others of the above named specialists may also be enlisted for teaching duties in some institutions. Teaching is thus a rather general characteristic of this group, but it cannot serve as a part of the definition for this professional-specialist group, since it is likely to be a voluntary function rather than one inherent in the position held.

[2]The present use of the word *specialist* is in a different sense from its use in *special librarianship,* where an active role in distillation, repackaging, and dissemination of information is implicit, and the meaning is distinctly different from *subject librarian.*

Another point of distinction is the special titles often used for these positions, titles assigned to make clear the special assignment which might not be evident from general classification, such as Librarian III or Principal Librarian. A special title may be granted because of the individual's exceptional background, his need for special designation in the community, or the administration's desire for a particular emphasis on the assignment. Thus the head of an audio-visual department may for clarity be called Chief of Audio-Visual Facilities or, possibly for emphasis, Director of Academic Communications and Instructional Media. One institution may prefer Chief of Photocopying Services, while another prefers Photographer to the Library, or Specialist for Documentary Reproduction. Yet here again, titles certainly cannot be used to help define the group though they may serve to show the prominence or administrative level of the position.

Professional-specialists may handle either traditional jobs or those rather recently added to the library; or they may direct newly formed departments or offices. Thus the position of Personnel Officer may be established when the constant tasks of staff recruitment and training reach proportions requiring that these functions be split off from others. Or new endowment income may serve to create a new position with responsibility for archives; and this assignment, combined, for example, with the library's need for a bibliographical project of distinction on a special collection, may result in the creation of a Division of Special Collections or a Department of Rare Books, Archives, and Manuscripts, with a chief or a curator to manage it. No one library will have many of each type within this specialist group, but great variations are possible. It must be concluded that the newness or the numbers of such positions do not help clarify the definition.

A close analysis of personnel policies and academic status will produce perhaps the only rather clear sign that a distinctive group does exist. In personnel policies the professional-specialist may be treated almost exactly as are the librarians, using whatever classification and enjoying whatever academic status are assigned to librarians within a given institution. Yet some differences can be detected, perhaps in salary schedules; or they may lie in eligibility rules for faculty benefits or other indications of status. Where this occurs, the variant treatment is almost certain to be because of their qualifications and services *intra muros* as professional specialists, often working especially closely with a department of instruction, rather than because they are librarians "with connections."

As a hypothetical case, an archivist may sit on university committees or be given standing in the university far beyond that of other library department heads when the university considers the archivist in a different light because of the especially important value of his services to the president, trustees, or alumni groups. Or the archivist may have been independent of the library until a recent reorganization; he may have been coordinate with the curator of the museum, the director of the press, or the director of libraries. Further, the business school, or the history and education departments, may have a special interest in the organization and use of the archive collection, and may use the archivist to give courses, to sit on committees, and to participate in their academic programs in other ways. The archivist in such an instance may have achieved special privileges by his own activities, competence, and personality combined with a set of local conditions.

Careful analysis of positions in each institution should show where the special nature of the appointment lies; the professional-specialist may by this definition have a slightly different treatment from the majority of librarians in one or another aspect of his employment. These aspects which will be briefly discussed are: the type of appointment, the classification of position, the salary schedule, the question of tenure, the availability of sabbaticals, and other perquisites.

1. *Type of appointment.* The specialist may hold a part-time appointment, even less than half-time, whereas the librarian is more frequently full time. He may have one or more jobs outside the university which occupy considerable time. Not infrequently a specialist may hold a joint appointment in the library and in another department of the university, either as an administrator or as a member of the instructional faculty. This mixed appointment for the professional-specialist might mean that he has two forms of status. He will have academic status and perhaps faculty rank for his library position; status deriving from another university appointment generally would be no improvement.

2. *Classification.* The professional-specialist will commonly be placed in the classification for librarians, the exact level being determined through job analysis, qualifications for candidacy, experience, and administrative responsibilities. An alternative might occasionally obtain where the specialist fills one of many similar positions existing elsewhere in the university. Thus, instead of the business manager being inserted into the library classification, he might in some institutions be included in a classification for other individuals having graduate business school training, when his qualifications are similar to those held by individuals in the controller's office or business office of the university. This latter pattern is certain to be the case with systems analysts, computer programmers, and probably with financial officers.

3. *Salary schedule.* Salaries are one place where the professional-specialist may be treated differently from librarians. The specialist is drawn from a different market which dictates the salary minimums for different levels. This creates a separate salary schedule *sui generis.* Where the specialist is a librarian who became a specialist by learning on the job, the salary schedule may be identical to that for other librarians. The personnel manager or the map librarian might be examples of this "in house" development. Others may be sought in a national market, such as an information

scientist, a photographic specialist, or an audio-visual specialist. Once the initial salary is established, the individual may enter at the appropriate level in the regular schedule for librarians, with normal consideration of salary increases following, unless the condition of the ·national market forces more substantial annual increases in order to hold the specialist.

It may be unfortunate that a preferential salary is sometimes determined by the demand and supply on the employment market. It is nevertheless unavoidable.[3] And to say that a financial advantage lacks equity with respect to the rest of the professional staff overlooks the fact that the specialist ran the risk of advanced training in a limited field. He invested time and funds to obtain an education for a field where relatively few are needed to fill positions in various types of organizations. Furthermore, any apparent stretching of salary scales on behalf of the specialist will only tend to bring other librarians along with him for improved salary, status, and benefits.

4. *Tenure.* The library part of his appointment will often, but not always, carry tenure if librarians are so covered. Even when the professional-specialist teaches one or more courses on a regular assignment in a department of instruction, he is not likely to gain faculty tenure for that unless it constitutes the major part of his appointment. In any event, his conditions for job security within the library would almost certainly be the same as those applying to other librarians.

5. *Sabbatical leaves.* As a specialist's job approaches the character of faculty occupations, his sabbatical arrangements should more closely resemble those of faculty than of business officers. That is, the professional-specialist in a scholarly or academic discipline who has achieved proficiency and a high status among his colleagues is probably able to demonstrate that he could profit from and make good use of a sabbatical leave. Thus some specialists, such as the paleographer, archivist, book selection specialist, or area curator may perhaps be in a more favorable position for a sabbatical than is the typical librarian, though the benefits of sabbatical leaves to all senior librarians can be argued very cogently.

6. *Other perquisites.* The professional-specialist is likely to have a slight advantage over the traditional librarian in such areas as faculty club membership, attendance with voting power at faculty meetings, housing privileges, travel funds, and automobile parking arrangements, though probably not in ticket priorities, tuition exemption for children, and insurance programs. This comes from the fact that he is a specialist in a minority group and a special case may be made for him without opening the flood gates. He may also have special arrangements with one or more departments of the university or with administrative offices which provide

---

[3]Evidence that the salary differential exists but is more modest than one might think is provided by Margo Trumpeter, "Non-Librarians in the Academic Library," *College and Research Libraries,* XXIX (November 1968), 461-65.

some leverage. Treatment can be unpredictable, however, and some may be at a disadvantage when compared with librarians.

Although a precise determination of who qualifies as a professional-specialist is not possible, it may be suggested that anywhere from 5 to as much as 20 per cent of the staff in some of the larger libraries would be specialists as described above. In most libraries it will probably be a smaller percentage. A library which needed specialists in past decades most often found them elsewhere than in library schools. Yet the trend toward employment of specialists has prompted graduate library schools in the past dozen years to organize institutes and add new courses and combination programs with other departments in the university in order to graduate librarians with better qualifications to handle unusual assignments.[4] It is clear that graduate library schools are increasingly meeting this need for specialists. Even so, many, if not most, of the professional-specialists are not required to obtain a graduate library degree. The educational requirements for holding such a position continue to be highly pragmatic; experience is the best recommendation.

The responsibilities of a few such positions and the qualifications sought in these appointments may be suggested in the following examples:

Space Coordinator, New York University Libraries: Involves the activities relating to library building projects, with particular emphasis on the coordination of interior space, layout, furnishings, and internal operating procedures and systems. The incumbent will act as liaison between the library administration and the various department heads, consultants, central university agencies and others involved in this project.

Details of duties to be performed include the setting up of calendars, assembling case materials, preparing minutes, preparing charts and sample layouts, maintaining current files and records of related activities, assisting in the preparation and distribution of public relations materials and a variety of administrative duties in direct support of the interior coordination of the library projects. Qualifications: degree in design, planning, or pre-architecture, and some experience in architectural or design office.

Librarian of East Asian Studies and Professor of Library Administration, Ohio State University Libraries: Graduate degree in library science from an accredited library school. Experience in selecting and cataloging East Asian library materials. Scholarly knowledge of the history and literature of the Chinese peoples and, to a lesser degree, of Japan and Korea. Knowledge of Chinese and Japanese languages.

Coordinator, Library Development Program, University of Tennessee Library: The coordinator for the library development program coordinates the university solicitation of books and manuscripts and money for books and

---

[4]See, for example, George S. Bonn, "Training and Education for Information Work," *American Documentation,* XIII (July 1962), 301-12.

manuscripts. The position requires a college degree, preferably a graduate degree. Teaching and research experience is highly desirable. A library science degree is not required, but would be desirable. A full acquaintanceship with the teaching and research needs of the institution itself is necessary; a wide knowledge of and enthusiasm for books requisite.

Research Associate in Statistical Services, University of Illinois Library: Library degree and some experience, preferably in technical services areas; interest in machine applications to library problems; ability to work well with people and to obtain cooperation from the library staff. Duties are to work with the library administration, departments involved in mechanizing procedures, the Statistical Services Unit, and advisory committees on library automation; recommend to the library administration specific equipment, programs, and procedures to be followed in the conversion to automation; work out the machine applications and oversee the actual conversion to machine operations of those programs approved by the library administration.

Head of Near Eastern Unit, University of Michigan Library: Has responsibility for the selection and cataloging of all materials in Near Eastern languages to be added to the university library collections, and assists in the acquisition of these materials. Qualifications: required are competence in Arabic, a working knowledge of one or more other languages in the area and of two major European languages and several years of library experience, especially with materials from the Near and Middle East and preferably including cataloging of vernacular materials; desirable are graduate degrees in Oriental studies and library science.

Chief of Administrative Services, Stanford University Libraries: College degree; graduate degree in or experience in business administration is considered of major importance; also important is knowledge of audio-visual, photographic, and data processing equipment and similar machine processes important to libraries; and useful is interest in studies of operational efficiency, in printing and publishing, and in building design and equipment. No graduate library school degree required. Minimum of five years experience in business or education is felt necessary.

The federal government has recently recognized the need for greater specialization in libraries. Under the 1966 U.S. Civil Service Commission "Position-Classification Standards: Librarian Series" (TS 60 p.19-20), positions as librarian may now be further defined by language or subject qualifications:

The following specializations are to be used (a) when the duties of the position require a knowledge of the basic principles, theories, practices, techniques, terminology and expressions of a discipline or specialized subject-matter area; or a comprehensive knowledge of one or more foreign languages sufficient to read library material fluently; *and* (b) when the need for such specialized subject-matter or language knowledges are a significant factor in the recruitment and assignment of personnel:

Subject-Matter Specializations

Biological Sciences	Business and Industry
Medical Sciences	Education
Physical Sciences	Fine Arts
Social Sciences	Humanities
Engineering	Law
Music	

Foreign Language Specializations

Arabic	Romance
Germanic	Slavic
Oriental	

Titles for individual positions should be constructed to reflect the specialized knowledges required to perform the work assigned. For example: Librarian (Social Sciences); Supervisory Librarian (Physical Sciences-Slavic Languages); Librarian (Romance Languages); Library Director (Law). When dual subject-matter specializations are required, these may be reflected in the title, *e.g.* Librarian (Fine Arts and Humanities).

There is undoubtedly a national trend for an increasing proportion of positions in university libraries to be specialist in character. There are large numbers of librarians who are full-time book selection specialists or curators of subject collections. Data processing specialists in university libraries are increasing in number. The use of personnel managers and business managers is increasing. And audio-visual divisions and photographic departments are now major enterprises in some institutions where they were embryonic twenty years ago.

Dean Harlow foresees that "many competent bit performers in a well ordered system (story tellers, abstractors, technicians, and subject specialists) do not require [the] extended perspective [of librarianship] and need not seek or be granted the freedom of the profession. Persons from allied professional fields, particularly sociology, political science, and technology, will play a major role in the decision-making processes of libraries ...."[5] This is a natural result of increasing size and complexity in university libraries. New qualifications are sought in appointments to help solve new problems. Many aspects of work in the larger university libraries can now profit by such specialized attention.

None of this is meant to imply that librarians will handle housekeeping chores while others will cope with the creative developments. Specialist-librarians will have major, often the most important, assignments. The shape of the future will depend in considerable measure on how graduate library schools respond to these

[5]Neal Harlow, "The Present Is Not What It Was," *Library Journal,* LXXXIX (June 15, 1964), 2531-32.

developments, and library schools are now doing a great deal better in offering specialization programs.[6]

Without resting a conclusion on fact, one may speculate that many types of professional-specialists will remain a part of library organizations in future decades. Some, such as the information scientists, may become an integral field within librarianship. Other specialists, perhaps the business manager and photographic specialists are examples, may always remain a clearly distinct group. One need only consider the officers of the Library of Congress to realize that large research libraries of the future are certain to have on the staff some men who are business specialists, lawyers, historians, as well as other specialists in editing, in communications, in audio systems, or in data processing.

This development is probably a sign of maturity in the library profession. It results from the fact that university libraries are now large and expensive enterprises requiring a staff with a high degree of sophisticated expertise.

[6]The need for improved library school offerings is little changed, only accentuated, since Dr. Charles C. Williamson wrote the chapter on "Advanced or Specialized Study" in *Training for Library Service: A Report Prepared for the Carnegie Corporation of New York* (New York, 1923), p. 91-102.

Academic
rank and status

Anita R. Schiller

Mrs. Schiller is Research Associate in the Library Research Center of the University of Illinois. This article, slightly revised, is taken from her *Characteristics of Professional Personnel in College and University Libraries* (Urbana: University of Illinois Library Research Center, May 1968; report no. BR5-0919; contract OEC-6-10-200).

The report from which this material is taken was based on a national survey of academic librarians employed in college and university libraries throughout the United States in 1966-67. Of 2,459 full-time professional staff sampled, 2,282 individuals (93 per cent) returned completed questionnaires.

Librarians are a small minority within the higher educational community; they constitute less than 3 per cent of all faculty and other professional staff in institutions of higher education.[1] Despite their crucial role in the educational process, their status has been somewhat anomalous.[2] Increasingly, the trend has been to recognize librarians on an equal basis with the teaching faculty by according them academic or faculty status and rank. This has been a gradual development, which has accelerated more recently as the importance of librarianship has come to be more widely acknowledged, and as librarians themselves have actively sought such recognition.

In 1959 the Association of College and Research Libraries, in an official statement of policy by its University Libraries Section, strongly recommended "that professional librarians be granted academic status, with corresponding faculty privileges."[3] Academic status is defined here as "the formal recognition

[1] U.S. Office of Education, *Faculty and Other Professional Staff, 1963-64*, (Washington: Dept. of Health, Education and Welfare, 1964) p.10

[2] For a collection of papers presenting various viewpoints and descriptions of the academic librarian's status, see Robert B. Downs, ed., *The Status of American College and University Librarians* (ACRL Monograph no. 22; Chicago: ALA, 1958). In "The Place of College Librarians in the Academic World," *California Librarian*, XXVIII (April 1967), 101-6, Downs emphasizes the case for faculty status and analyzes the major reasons for it.

[3] "Status of College and University Librarians," *College and Research Libraries*, XX (September 1959), 399. These privileges "relate to tenure, academic freedom, sabbatical leaves, equitable salaries, holidays, insurance, and retirement." *Ibid.*, 400.

in writing, by an institution's authorities, of librarians as members of the instructional and research staff. The recognition may take the form of assigned faculty ranks and titles, or equivalent ranks and titles, according to institutional customs."[4] The "ALA Standards for College Libraries" state that "professional librarians should have faculty status, with the benefits enjoyed by the teaching staff";[5] and the "ALA Standards for Junior College Libraries" call for faculty status for professional librarians, "preferably including faculty rank and titles identical to those of the teaching staff" and the benefits which faculty status involves.[6]

ACADEMIC RANK

The present survey sought to determine the extent to which librarians hold academic rank, which ranks they hold, and what factors are associated with rank. The pertinent questions from the survey requested information only on academic *rank,* not on the related but hard-to-define concept of *status.* The tables in the first section below pertain, therefore, only to rank. The second half of the chapter, which consists largely of comments from respondents on the questions concerning rank, shows that many academic librarians are also concerned with other aspects of faculty status.

Table 1
FACULTY RANK, BY SEX
(PER CENT DISTRIBUTION)

Faculty Rank	Total	Men	Women
No rank	48.8%	45.2%	51.0%
Instructor	20.9	16.5	23.4
Assistant professor	16.5	18.6	15.2
Associate professor	7.0	8.6	6.0
Professor	4.6	9.3	2.0
Other rank, or rank not specified	2.2	1.8	2.4
Total	100.0%	100.0%	100.0%
Base	2254	828	1426

The findings of this survey show that only slightly over half of all academic librarians hold faculty rank. Of all the respondents, 20.9 per cent are classified with the rank or equivalent rank of instructor, 16.5 per cent as assistant professor, 7.0 per cent as associate professor, and 4.6 per cent as professor. "Other rank," such as lecturer, and "rank not specified" together constitute 2.2 per cent of all the respondents. This category includes those who had been granted

[4]*Ibid.*
[5]"ALA Standards for College Libraries," *College and Research Libraries,* XX (July 1959), 276.
[6]"ALA Standards for Junior College Libraries," *College and Research Libraries,* XXI (May 1960), 202.

academic rank very recently, but were not yet sure which rank they held. Taking together all the foregoing classifications, those with rank constitute 51.2 per cent of the respondents. Those who noted that they did not hold a specific faculty rank, but had some form of status, are included in the category "no rank" in the above table.

Relatively more men than women reported that they hold faculty rank, but the differences in their representation at specific levels of rank are much more pronounced. Women are more likely than men, for example, to hold the rank of instructor, but they are relatively less likely than men to hold appointments as assistant professor or above. At the full professor level, men outnumber women both relatively and absolutely. Although the majority of librarians are women, three quarters of those who are full professors are men. Altogether, only 105 individuals, or less than 5 per cent of the 2,254 respondents reporting, hold this rank. Compared to an estimated 30 per cent of total full-time faculty in degree-granting institutions who are full professors,[7] the proportion of librarians (9.3 per cent of the men, and 2.0 per cent of the women) who hold this rank seems particularly small.

Other Relevant Factors

Faculty rank for librarians is associated with a variety of other factors, as the following tables indicate. Teachers colleges, for example, are more likely than other types of institutions to grant faculty rank.

Table 2
FACULTY RANK, BY TYPE OF INSTITUTION WHERE EMPLOYED
(PER CENT DISTRIBUTION)

Faculty Rank	Total	Type of Institution				
		Teachers College	Liberal Arts College	Two yr. Insti-tution	Other Prof. School	University
Yes	51.2%	70.5%	58.8%	55.4%	42.9%	42.7%
No	48.8	29.5	41.2	44.6	57.1	57.3
Total	100.0%	100.0%	100.0%	100.0%	100.0%	100.0%
Base	2254	217	641	213	133	1050

Public institutions offer faculty rank more readily than do those under private control, but church-related institutions are even more likely to do so than public institutions. (It is not clear, however, whether such variations may be accounted for by differences in institutional philosophy or by other factors, such as institutional size.)

[7]"Sampling Study of the Teaching Faculty in Higher Education," *NEA Research Bulletin*, XLIV (February 1966), 8.

Table 3
FACULTY RANK, BY CONTROL OF
INSTITUTION WHERE EMPLOYED
(PER CENT DISTRIBUTION)

Faculty Rank	Total	Public	Private	Private Church-Related	Private Inde-pendent
				Control of Institution	
Yes	51.2%	56.5%	44.0%	60.1%	31.3%
No	48.8	43.5	56.0	39.9	68.7
Total	100.0%	100.0%	100.0%	100.0%	100.0%
Base	2254	1293	961	424	537

By position level, chief librarians are more apt than others to hold faculty rank.

Table 4
FACULTY RANK, BY POSITION LEVEL
(PER CENT DISTRIBUTION)

Faculty Rank	Total	Chief Libn.	Asst. Libn.	Dept. or Division Head, etc.*	Other Prof. Asst.
Yes	51.2%	64.2%	58.1%	51.7%	43.7%
No	48.8	35.8	41.9	48.3	56.3
Total	100.0%	100.0%	100.0%	100.0%	100.0%
Base	2251	341	234	813	863

*Includes head of college, school, or departmental library.

As indicated earlier, relatively more men than women reported that they hold faculty rank.

Table 5
FACULTY RANK, BY SEX
(PER CENT DISTRIBUTION)

Faculty Rank	Total	Men	Women
Yes	51.2%	54.8%	49.0%
No	48.8	45.2	51.0
Total	100.0%	100.0%	100.0%
Base	2254	828	1426

Those with the basic professional degree are somewhat more likely than others to hold faculty rank, although over two fifths of those without this degree have faculty rank.

Table 6
FACULTY RANK, BY WHETHER RESPONDENT HAS
PROFESSIONAL LIBRARY DEGREE
(PER CENT DISTRIBUTION)

Faculty Rank		Total	Has Professional Library Degree	
			Yes	No
Yes		51.2%	52.5%	44.8%
No		48.8	47.5	55.2
	Total	100.0%	100.0%	100.0%
	Base	2240	1874	366

Considering each of the foregoing factors, formal teaching activities seem particularly important. Of all the sampled librarians, just slightly over half hold faculty rank, but of those 324 respondents who teach one or more credit courses, nearly four fifths (78.4 per cent), hold faculty rank.

Table 7
FACULTY RANK, BY WHETHER RESPONDENT
TEACHES CREDIT COURSES
(PER CENT DISTRIBUTION)

Faculty Rank		Total	Teaches Credit Courses	
			Yes	No
Yes		51.1%	78.4%	46.5%
No		48.9	21.6	53.5
	Total	100.0%	100.0%	100.0%
	Base	2234	324	1910

Another factor which is closely associated with rank is the doctoral degree. Of 81 respondents reporting on faculty rank and holding a doctorate in library science or in any other field, 75 per cent have faculty rank. Furthermore, the rank of full professor is the dominant one for this group. Of the 81 respondents with a doctorate, 40 per cent are full professors, 35 per cent are in all other ranks combined, and 25 per cent have no rank. In the sample at large, however, less than 5 per cent of the respondents are full professors.[8]

[8]Describing the need for recognition of college mathematics teachers who lack the PhD degree, a report by a committee of the American Mathematics Association states: "Un-

Types of Appointment Other than Rank

Although the survey questionnaire requested an indication of academic rank only, several hundred respondents who do not hold academic rank voluntarily cited other types of classification which they hold. Below are some illustrations of the various types of appointments reported by respondents who do not hold a specific academic rank:

> no formal title; not specified; state civil service rank; administrative staff; administrative faculty; officer of administration; coadjutant administration; considered part of administration; officer; corporation appointment; Regent's appointment; one under the academic dean's office; academic staff; non-teaching faculty; extra-ordinary faculty; academician; semi-academic; academic, but not faculty; staff; staff member; staff associate, professional librarian; librarian—a rank in itself, I suppose; Librarian (highest rank for librarian on campus); Librarian I, Librarian II, (etc.); our positions are called professional and we are called faculty members, but we are in a class by ourselves.

LIBRARIANS SPEAK OUT ON RANK AND STATUS

Judging from the freely offered comments of many respondents to the present survey, rank and status are regarded as major issues by academic librarians. These spontaneous comments were so numerous, they illuminated so many aspects of this issue, and they expressed such strong convictions, that they were considered important enough to cite here in some detail. The following comments, therefore, are offered as examples of what the respondents themselves chose to write about. Full faculty status for librarians is apparently a particularly urgent concern:

> The single most unsatisfactory condition of my employment is the lack of any type of faculty status.

> Our biggest gripe here concerns our "faculty status." In any academic procession we fall at the end of the line either just before or just after the graduate assistants.

> Two great problems face many university librarians: a) lack of faculty status and b) lack of any grievance and appeals procedure.

> College and university librarians should have all benefits enjoyed by the teaching faculty. Academic rank is a must.

> Faculty status should be stressed for college and university librarians.

> Librarians at ——— are classified as staff members and as such are subject to

---

fortunately, the relevance of the doctoral degree in the qualification of a college teacher is often misunderstood, and the resulting confusion has, in many cases, led to serious abuses. We have in mind such abuses as the preferential treatment frequently assured the holder of a doctoral degree over an otherwise well-qualified teacher who lacks a Ph.D." Quoted by Luther J. Carter in "Shortage of Mathematics Teachers: Seeking Status for the Non-Ph.D.," *Science,* CLIX (March 8, 1968), 1082.

the same rules as the janitors and kitchen help, i.e., no tenure, two weeks vacation, barred from using certain facilities on campus.

This library is so completely unorganized that one doubts his status. The librarian . . . has faculty status. The assistant's position is more of a glorified flunky.

Here at ——— gymnastic teachers and swimming instructors—not to speak of football and baseball coaches—hold higher ranks than librarians and get their promotions earlier and faster.

Few respondents volunteered dissent from the principle of faculty status. Their comments are cited below:

Academic librarians make a great to-do about status, particularly faculty status; but they forget that professors profess, and librarians serve, and there is a historical difference of long standing. . . . There are amenities which professional librarians ought to work for but rank status is another matter.

There are too many professional librarians here for the size of the library and the type of work that is done. Librarians do not deserve faculty status unless they have higher degrees in other subject fields.

Librarians wanting to be recognized as a valuable profession should improve themselves, not their positions.

Others pointed to specific reasons why equal status with the teaching faculty is important. Several believed their educational preparation equalled or exceeded that of many nonlibrary faculty. Other reasons also were given:

We here are currently in "Limbo," neither faculty rank nor status. Thus, we are involved directly with curriculum and instruction, but have no voting privileges—nor do we attend faculty meetings . . . .

Faculty status would be an asset in smoothing relations between librarians and faculty members.

Librarians . . . work as hard, if not harder, than many of the faculty members. It is high time that we be treated accordingly.

The librarian of any special collection has to be a scholar, too, but the professional status in the academic world and the actual financial compensation are too low to attract qualified and conscientious workers.

Another respondent viewed the librarian's lack of status within the broader context of the role of higher educational institutions.

The University, which likes to think of itself as a leader, is far behind the times concerning librarians. . . . Academic rank and better salaries for librarians are essential. . . . The University administration must soon realize this and do something about it.

Some librarians mentioned that academic status currently is being sought or is in the process of being granted:

We are trying to get faculty status this year, by working through our librarian.

I am also a member of TACT (Texas Association of College Teachers), which is also trying to get faculty status for librarians.

The academic status of professional librarians at ——— is under consideration.

Academic status has just been granted to professional librarians at ———.

Now called academic, but exact meaning being clarified at this time.

Occasionally, faculty status is accompanied by other faculty perquisites, even where there is no stated designation of faculty rank:

We do not have rank but we do have status and are voting members of the faculty council.

Academic status, with University Senate membership (but no faculty title).

Have faculty status . . . (retirement program, membership in Academic Senate), but no assigned equivalent teaching rank.

Since my salary is based on a straight academic schedule, since I attend and vote in faculty meetings and am accorded all privileges of an instructor, I presume that this amounts to academic rank, in our small and informal school.

I am considered a member of the faculty and am entitled to such privileges as a sabbatical, but I have no academic rank like professor, instructor, etc.

Much more frequently, however, those with faculty or academic status, but who do not have faculty rank, consider that their status is "meaningless" and "vague," and that it brings with it no guarantee of equal benefits:

Issue is currently being kicked around. We have "academic status" but no one is sure just what this means.

We are vaguely classified as "faculty."

We have been told that we have academic status. I do not know that this is officially stated in any university policy.

Faculty status of librarians should be clarified. We have it in name but have no rank nor faculty salaries nor faculty vacations, etc.

It is purely a name and carries with it no academic responsibilities or privileges or guarantees.

"Academic status," [an] administrative-jargon-word made up to keep librarians happy. (This aim has not been accomplished.)

Being told I have "faculty status" is not necessarily the same thing as being considered and treated as a faculty member. Faculty status for librarians who do not teach evidently means what the administration decides it will mean—no more, no less. This sort of situation can be disappointing, to say the least.

Rank No, Status Yes. HA!

We are called faculty, but not same privileges or pay.

We have faculty privileges, but not faculty salaries.

Librarians have academic status, but are not members of the policy body, the academic senate.

We are considered as professionals when the administration wants something, but the corresponding privileges are not accorded.

Many of those without academic rank did mention specific privileges to which they were entitled, but frequently these privileges seem to represent a symbolic or token form of recognition rather than genuinely equal status:

No academic rank but do attend faculty meetings (without vote).

Not [academic rank] specifically, although I am invited to faculty committee.

No [rank] but position is given faculty respect, amenities and consideration.

No, but we're permitted to go to faculty club.

Some faculty privileges (dining hall, etc.).

In academic processions [we] walk with assistant professors.

We are permitted to belong to the faculty club.

We, with others of administrative staff, may use faculty parking lot and eat at faculty club.

Several respondents indicated that when academic rank is conferred in their institution, it is based on some factor other than their professional position in the library.

Librarians are given academic rank here only if they teach at least 3 credit hours; the orientation class is only 1 credit hour.

As librarian "no," as director of program in library science, "yes."

No, my library position has no academic rank. I am assistant professor of law as a lawyer, not as a librarian.

Academic rank based primarily on academic training. Library position and academic rank not necessarily related.

Thus, librarians may be classified as faculty, with faculty rank and faculty benefits, or they may be classified in other ways. They may have the title but not the perquisites; they may have the perquisites but not the title; some have neither; some have both. In some institutions part of the professional library staff is classified in one way, and part of it in another, and only certain positions, such as chief librarian, or certain individuals, such as those with particular educatonal qualifications or those with classroom teaching responsibilities, are accorded faculty rank.

Varying institutional policy toward teaching faculty accounts for some of the variations in the way librarians are classified. Not all institutions provide the same faculty benefits, and some institutions do not assign specific ranks to members of the teaching faculty. Furthermore, the standards of the regional higher educational accrediting associations do not uniformly require faculty standing and privileges for all professional library staff.[9] Whatever privileges and benefits are extended to nonlibrary faculty in individual institutions, however, they are not always offered to librarians in the same measure. The status of librarians is often ill defined, and their privileges may be even more uncertain. Academic librarians are concerned about both.

SALARY BY FACULTY RANK

The median salary of $8,260 for librarians who hold faculty rank is higher than the median salary of $7,537 for librarians without faculty rank (table 8). Faculty rank therefore appears to confer a salary advantage. This is particularly apparent at the higher ranks, for median salary rises with each level of faculty rank to $12,370 for those who are full professors. It is also noteworthy, however, that the median salary for librarians with the rank of instructor ($7,250) is somewhat less than that for librarians who do not hold faculty rank ($7,537).

Table 8
MEDIAN ANNUAL SALARY BY FACULTY RANK, BY SEX
(PER CENT DISTRIBUTION)

Faculty Rank	Total		Men		Women	
	Per Cent	Median Salary	Per Cent	Median Salary	Per Cent	Median Salary
Without rank	49.2	$7,537	45.6	$8,730	51.3	$7,285
With rank	50.8	8,260	54.4	9,220	48.7	7,815
Instructor	20.8	7,250	16.6	7,540	23.3	7,130
Asst. professor	16.5	8,765	18.8	9,160	15.1	8,535
Assoc. professor	6.9	10,360	8.5	11,270	6.0	9,445
Professor	4.5	12,730	8.9	14,330	1.9	9,750
Has rank, but not specified*	2.1	7,750	1.6	9,000	2.4	7,333
Total	100.0%	$7,931**	100.0%	$8,983**	100.0%	$7,460**
Base	2157		799		1358	

*Includes lecturers.
**Median for those reporting rank.

Earlier sections of this paper reported a strong association between formal teaching responsibilities and faculty rank. It is not unexpected to find, therefore, that those librarians who teach formal courses tend to earn more than those who do not. The median salary for the former group is $9,230, while the median salary for those with no formal teaching responsibilities (this group constitutes 86 per cent of 2,153 individuals reporting salary) is $7,745.

[9]Fritz Veit, "The Status of the Librarian According to Accrediting Standards of Regional and Professional Associations," *College and Research Libraries,* XXI (March 1969), 127-35.

In *The Academic Marketplace,* Caplow and McGee point to an interesting paradox. They claim that

> For most members of the teaching professions, the real strain in the academic role arises from the fact that they are, in essence, paid to do one job, whereas the worth of their services is evaluated on the basis of how well they do another. . . Most professors contract to perform teaching services. .· . . When they are evaluated, however, either as candidates for a vacant position, or as candidates for promotion, the evaluation is made principally in terms of their research contributions to their disciplines.[10]

It seems particularly ironic, therefore, to note that although librarians are employed to perform library activities, they seem to be evaluated, at least where salary or rank is concerned, on the basis of their formal teaching activities.

Some institutions have begun to take more seriously the librarian's educational role, to recognize the importance of this role regardless of formal classroom teaching responsibilities, and to bring librarians' salaries more closely into line with other faculty salaries. In some cases this recognition has resulted in part from the strong position taken by librarians themselves. At the City University of New York, where professional librarians have full faculty status, including faculty titles and salaries, the "first library rank now carries the title Instructor with a salary range from $8,100 to $11,950."[11] Even here, however, where librarians are "entitled to sabbatical leave, and all the other benefits and responsibilities of faculty membership," they are not entitled to equal annual vacation.[12]

[10]Theodore Caplow and Reece J. McGee, *The Academic Marketplace* (New York: Basic Books, Inc., 1958), p.82.

[11]"Librarians Get Faculty Status at City University of New York," *Library Journal,* XCI (January 15, 1966), 219.

[12]*Ibid.,* 220.

The status of California state college librarians

This report was prepared by an ALA ad hoc *committee appointed by President William S. Dix in September 1969. The committee consisted of Norman D. Alexander, Director, Southern Oregon University Library; Archie L. McNeal, Director, University of Miami Library; Philip J. McNiff, Director, Boston Public Library; and Robert B. Downs, Dean of Library Administration, University of Illinois, chairman.*

The controversy over the place of professional librarians in the California State Colleges has been simmering for nearly two decades, at times boiling over, and there is little doubt that the dispute will continue until major differences are resolved.

In an effort to discover whether any common ground could be found between the librarians and the administration of the State College system, and possibly to serve as arbitrators, President William Dix in September 1969 appointed a committee of the American Library Association to confer with Chancellor Dumke and Assistant Chancellor Keene and with representatives of the State College librarians. Meetings were held in Los Angeles on October 13-14. In the committee's judgment, the differences are far from irreconcilable, everyone is anxious to bring the prolonged discussions to a satisfactory conclusion, and there is an evident willingness on both sides to accept reasonable compromises.

An analysis of the "Position Paper on Status and Benefits for Librarians in California's Colleges and Universities," issued by an *ad hoc* committee of the California Library Association's College, University, and Research Library Section, shows that the librarians are asking for full faculty status with appropriate ranks; salary scales identical to the teaching faculty, with suitable additional compensation for twelve-month appointments; assignments to professional tasks only; time for independent research and other professional activities; sabbatical and other leaves; security of employment and tenure; appointments and promotions based on standards comparable to those of members of the teaching faculty; eligibility for grants, fellowships, and research funds; access to the faculty grievance, appeal, and review procedures; and membership in the Academic Senates. In a later statement there was also proposed "Participation of all librarians in library governance."

The validity of a majority of the points enumerated above would be widely accepted. Some of them will be considered in detail below. Given the critical financial situation in which the California State Colleges find themselves at present, however, the best that can be expected will be to have certain demands approved in principle without immediate implementation. In this category fall the matters which would require the allocation of considerable additional funds to the libraries, such as equivalent faculty salary scales, with supplementary pay for year-round appointments; time off for research and other professional activities; sabbaticals and other leaves with pay; and grants, fellowships and research funds.

The librarians with whom the ALA Committee discussed the list of demands recognized the existing financial stringency and appeared agreeable to the idea of later implementation, when conditions are more favorable, if agreement in principle can be reached now. Meanwhile, as long as prospects are good for endorsement of the program in general by the State College system administration, the committee would consider it unwise for the librarians to promote further the idea of censure and sanctions. Such a confrontation and hardening of positions would create an exceedingly difficult atmosphere in which to reach any agreement.

Further examination of specific points included in the librarians' position paper is in order. First, and from a long-range point of view most important, is the question of faculty status for professional librarians.

FACULTY STATUS

The trend throughout the United States and Canada, especially in public colleges and universities, is running strongly in the direction of full academic status for librarians. A recent survey of the university members of the Association of Research Libraries revealed that with few exceptions professional librarians in those institutions have academic or faculty status. Among the states to which the nation customarily looks for educational leadership, California is most backward in this respect. Here, neither the State Colleges nor the University of California recognizes librarians as faculty members. In contrast, in the state of Illinois, for example, all of the state senior colleges and universities have granted faculty status to their professional librarians. Prerogatives which accompany this recognition include tenure, rank, voting rights, retirement benefits, group insurance, and frequently sabbatical and study leaves. The publicly supported institutions in New York City and State are following the same pattern.

The market for professional librarians is national and even international in scope, and for the past twenty-five years it has been a seller's market. A shortage of well-qualified librarians is likely to continue into the indefinite future. A competent librarian will have numerous job opportunities. There is a free flow of librarians across state lines and among types of libraries. The enterprising and ambitious librarian is unlikely to remain where his status is unsatisfactory and perquisites substandard. The institutions that will be most successful in attracting and holding able staff members are those in which librarians are recognized as an integral part of the academic ranks, a vital group in the educational process, with high qualifications for appointment and all the rights and privileges of other academic employees.

On the other hand, if the professional librarians are in some nondescript category, without clearly defined status, with no institutional understanding of the contributions which they can make to the educational program, and if they are placed outside of or made ineligible for the usual academic prerogatives, the library will have serious difficulty in recruiting or retaining staff members of more than average ability.

It should be stressed that satisfactory status for its librarians brings important benefits to an institution, not merely to the librarians. The quality of a college or university can be judged by looking at its library. If an institution's library is weak, the institution itself is mediocre. The better the library, the stronger the faculty the college will be able to hold and the higher-quality students it will attract. A prime criterion in judging the strength of a library is the quality and status of the library staff. Without a competent staff the library will offer inferior services, falling below its best potentialities.

Anyone who views the matter objectively must conclude that the participation of librarians in the educational program justifies their inclusion in the academic category. Supporting the claim for academic or faculty status for professional librarians is the fact that librarians are teachers, formally or informally. As described in a study of the City University of New York:

> The instruction performed by librarians in both classroom teaching and extra-classroom teaching. This activity may be grouped into the following categories: (1) lectures on the use of the library and library research tools, given to students of all levels in visits to classrooms; (2) lecture-demonstrations to particular groups in the library, at the request of colleagues on the faculty; (3) the preparation of teaching aids, supplementary to textbooks— such as annotated reading lists and guides to particular kinds of material in the library; (4) the preparation of visual aids, supplementary to classroom lectures—such as films, tape recordings, and displays; (5) individual conferences with advanced students on their problems with term papers, honors papers, and theses; (6) education of prospective librarians; (7) participation in teaching programs, such as general studies and adult education, in addition to regular professional work.

But even if librarians never enter a classroom, their right to be called teachers is entirely legitimate. Librarians are contributing in fundamental fashion through developing and making available resources for study and research to the primary purposes for which institutions of higher education are founded. Able reference librarians require thorough knowledge of the contents of a great variety of books, journals, pamphlets, and unpublished data to carry on their work. Among acquisition librarians and subject catalogers are linguists and experts in various fields.

Despite the foregoing considerations, objections to faculty status for librarians are sometimes voiced on the ground that they are academically un-qualified. The criticism should be examined.

Some fields have tended to emphasize the doctorate more than others. Librarians are in the company of engineers, lawyers, artists, musicians, and certain other groups who belong to the university or college community but who in the past have customarily followed different patterns of training. In the library field, it should be noted, the situation is gradually changing as more and more schools offer the doctorate in library science. Instead of the doctorate, many librarians hold two master's degrees, ordinarily one in library science and the other in a subject field. The combination may be of more value to a practicing librarian than too narrow specialization.

In any case, one must recognize merit in the contention that librarians should establish their place in the academic world by proper preparation. Like the teaching profession, librarianship is becoming increasingly a career for specialists and its requirements are diverse. The librarians of the future will be expected to possess academic preparation as thorough and as advanced as their colleagues in other fields. The criteria normally considered in faculty promotions should also be applied to librarians, such as professional writing and publication, research in library science, participation in the activities of professional associations, bibliographical instruction to students at all levels, and aid to individual faculty research.

A 1967 survey of the academic qualifications of librarians in the California State Colleges reported that nearly 100 per cent held master's degrees in library science, 13 per cent had additional master's degrees, about 5 per cent held doctorates in addition to master's degrees in library science, and more than 42 per cent had engaged in advanced study. Furthermore, 29 per cent had teaching experience, 47 per cent had given occasional lectures, and 43 per cent had experience in teaching research techniques. About one third of the total group had publications on their records, and 91 per cent of the college librarians had published. A high percentage of the librarians was active in professional associations. An updated study would doubtless show further advances in all these areas.

RECOMMENDATION

It is the unanimous recommendation of the ALA Committee that professional librarians in the California State College system be granted full faculty status as expeditiously as possible. As a first step in this direction, it is suggested that the Academic Senate of the California State Colleges be asked to reconsider its action of October 20, 1967, reading as follows:

> Resolution "Status and Benefits for Librarians," urging the Chancellor and the Trustees to establish faculty equivalent classification for salary, but without the ascription of rank and class; standards of degrees and professional competence to be equivalent to professors; promotions based on professional merit; sabbatical and research leaves with pay, and other faculty fringe benefits; and academic year appointments for librarians.

The wording of the resolution is constructive and commendable in all except one particular, and the single flaw could be fatal to the librarians' cause: "but without the ascription of rank and class." Faculty status without rank or titles is largely meaningless, as librarians in other institutions have discovered on the basis of sad experience. It should be proposed to the senate that it substitute "and with" for the words "but without" in the resolution, to put the support of the senate behind the librarians' recommendation for full faculty status.

In its 1967 position paper, the CLA *ad hoc* Committee on Academic Status proposed that "the holding of academic rank shall be independent of the holding of administrative positions in the library." That principle may be valid except for the chief librarians, for whom high ranks should be provided in order to attract the ablest individuals. Otherwise, rank ought to be based on such factors as academic qualifications, experience, importance of assignments, scholarly interests, and individual merit.

It is recommended further that all professional librarians presently in the State College system be ranked, regardless of level, from instructor to professor, according to the criteria indicated. For purposes of staff morale and *esprit de corps*, complete reorganization at one time is preferable to a gradual approach.

SALARIES

Librarians are asking for "the same salaries for an academic year as do other faculty members in the same ranks," and further, "where librarians are offered 12 month appointments, their salaries will be adjusted on the same basis as other faculty members." Certainly, whatever minima are established for various faculty ranks should be applicable also to librarians. For example, if a minimum salary is set for assistant professors, librarians with the rank of assistant professor should receive no less. The colleges' financial difficulties, previously discussed, may preclude, however, the immediate correction of inequities between the salaries of librarians and other members of the faculty. The adjustments may require a period of time to work out.

The same problem arises in connection with the proposal for academic year appointments and supplementary pay for twelve-month appointments. Without a large increase in staffs, the libraries could hardly operate if all librarians were on academic year appointments. A satisfactory solution to this problem was found nearly twenty-five years ago in the University of Illinois Library: librarians' basic salaries are for the academic year, but almost without exception appointments are for twelve months, with two-ninths additional salary (equivalent to the salary for an eight-week summer session appointment).

RECOMMENDATION

It is recommended that (1) California State College librarians continue to receive twelve-month appointments, with a minimum of one-month vacation, (2) base salaries be for the academic year with minima the same as for the teaching faculty, and (3) in recognition of the longer period of service expected of librarians, they receive supplementary salaries based on a percentage of the academic year salaries.

LIBRARIANS' OTHER DEMANDS

If the librarians were granted full faculty status, a majority of other points included in the position paper would follow automatically, *e.g.*, sabbaticals and other paid leaves (somewhat theoretical at present because of lack of funds); eligibility for grants, fellowships, and research funds; security of employment and tenure; appointments and promotions based on standards comparable to those governing the teaching faculty; access to the faculty grievance, appeal, and review procedures; and membership in the academic senates of the individual campuses.

Somewhat ambiguous and difficult to define is the proposal that librarians be granted "time for independent research and other professional activities." Questions which may legitimately be raised include the following: Does this mean an abbreviated workweek, and if so, can the library's operations be carried on without substantial additions to the staff? How many members of the staffs are interested in and qualified to do "research"? (The experience elsewhere demonstrates that a small percentage of librarians are research minded.) What is meant by "other professional activities"?

RECOMMENDATION

It is recommended that (1) librarians in the system be granted time to attend professional meetings with travel expenses paid (if in accord with college policy); (2) time off or reduced work schedules be arranged for librarians who present specific research projects which they wish to pursue; (3) the librarians' workweek be as flexible as efficient library operation will permit, eliminating any aspect of time-clock punching; (4) librarians be granted leaves for advanced study and to complete approved research projects; and (5) time allowances be made for attendance at on-campus courses which would strengthen the librarians' preparation for their work, *e.g.,* foreign languages, computer technology, advanced statistics.

In summary, the ALA Committee's principal recommendations affecting the California State College librarians are these:

1. All librarians should be granted full faculty status as quickly as possible.
2. The principle should be accepted, and implemented as soon as feasible, that the salaries of librarians are to be equated with the teaching faculty, beginning with the establishment of minimum salaries for various ranks.
3. Librarians will continue to be on twelve-month appointments, but base salaries will be for the academic year, with a supplementary stipend for the longer period of service.
4. The professional growth of librarians will be aided and encouraged by grants of time and travel expense for attendance at professional meetings, reduced work loads for staff members engaged in research projects, flexible schedules, leaves for advanced study and research, and time to attend pertinent on-campus courses and lectures.

The visiting committee is convinced that if the foregoing recommendations are adopted in principle and in substance the California State College system's library personnel problems will be resolved on all major issues. It should also be noted that the University of California's nine campuses are confronted with similar difficulties and it would therefore be helpful to California's entire system of public higher education if the State Colleges would assume the leadership in finding satisfactory solutions.

The status of librarians in four-year state colleges and universities

Raj Madan, Eliese Hetler, and Marilyn H. Strong

Mrs. Madan and Mrs. Hetler are Associate Librarians and Miss Strong is Head of Reference at the Library of the State University of New York College at Brockport. Their report was published in *College and Research Libraries,* September 1968.

This study developed from the efforts of librarians at the four-year campuses and university centers of the State University of New York to gain complete faculty status. The paper is based on the replies from a questionnaire sent to 321 four-year state colleges and university centers across the United States. The compilation of statistics is based on a 57 per cent return. Status for librarians was equated with that of the academic faculties in regard to rank and titles, promotion criteria, tenure, sabbatical leave, rates of pay, holidays and vacations, participation in faculty government, and fringe benefits.

The college librarian is no longer regarded (if he ever was) as simply a keeper of musty collections of books. He has had to make his own contributions to the new methods of information dissemination and to new approaches to research and teaching. As academic requisites have risen through the years, the qualifications of librarians have had to keep pace with the demands of the academic world of the twentieth century. In a number of colleges and universities throughout the country the librarian is now, as a result, accepted as a member of the faculty, with concomitant duties and responsibilities. He teaches, conducts research, publishes, serves on important faculty committees, and often occupies an influential seat in the faculty senate.

This is true, however, of only a very limited number of schools. In most places, the college librarian has remained in academic limbo. He has heeded the rapidly increasing demands for better training, greater specialization, and more versatility, but his own demands for equal status have not been accorded the same attention. The results have been what one might have expected. In those colleges and

95

universities where equality of status is not granted, the college librarian has become a scarce commodity, a vanishing species. Despite some breakthroughs, progress toward equality of status has been exceedingly slow. Robert B. Downs, in a 1958 monograph, was able to report only little progress throughout the country in the direction of improved status.[1] Nine years later, R. Dean Galloway wrote:

> A college can no more achieve excellence without an excellent faculty. In fact, it can't even build an excellent faculty without first having an excellent library. Yet the architect of library excellence—the professional librarian—has been so neglected that there is now an acute national shortage, and in most college libraries there is a crisis in recruiting qualified librarians. This crisis is a result of a failure throughout the years to grant status and benefits to librarians that are commensurate with their qualifications and their duties.[2]

As if to prove the truth of Dr. Galloway's statement, the monolithic State University of New York that same spring made an announcement of salary increases that were significantly smaller for librarians than for teaching faculties, despite the fact that State University of New York is plagued with the usual critical shortage of qualified librarians.

The State University of New York system employs about four hundred professional librarians at its twenty-eight colleges and universities.[3] Inequities in status exist on every campus. Administrators apply the same criteria for librarians' promotions as they do for the teaching faculty, yet they are usually considered as part of the administrative staff, without the rights and privileges of the academics. The ferment for improved status has, however, resulted in the formation of working committees at most of the campuses, and their combined efforts have yielded some results.

In October 1967 the faculty senate of the State University of New York recommended that professional librarians be granted faculty status without faculty titles but with all rights, privileges, and obligations thereof. The senate advised its executive committee to prepare the necessary amendments for the policies of the board of trustees. Further, in its report of February 1968 the State University of New York faculty senate recommended that members of the professional staff of State University of New York libraries be accorded academic appointments and tenure by 1970. These recommendations were approved in total on June 12, by the board of trustees.

---

[1] Robert B. Downs, ed., *The Status of American College and University Librarians* (ACRL Monograph no. 22; Chicago: ALA, 1958).

[2] R. Dean Galloway, "Academic Benefits for Academic Librarians, " *AAUP Bulletin,* LIII (Spring 1967), 61.

[3] The twenty-eight colleges of the SUNY system consists of four university centers, twelve specialized colleges, two medical centers, and ten four-year colleges. The junior colleges are not included since they operate under different administrative policies.

The writers of this article, members of the *ad hoc* committee on faculty status for librarians at the State University College at Brockport, New York (one of ten colleges of arts and sciences in the SUNY system) recently conducted a nation-wide survey of four-year colleges and universities to determine the present status of librarians on other state university campuses throughout the country. In preparation for the survey, the following definition of "full faculty status" for librarians was formulated:

> "Faculty status" entails complete equality with the academic faculty in regard to rank and titles, promotion criteria, tenure, sabbatical leave, rates of pay, holidays and vacations, representation and participation in faculty government and fringe benefits.

Only when equality in all the above conditions was met did we consider that librarians should be regarded as having "full faculty status."

THE QUESTIONNAIRE[4]

The survey was limited to four-year state colleges and universities because the committee wanted to compare its situation with sister state institutions throughout the country. New York State four-year colleges and university centers were excluded from the study since recent data were available from a study conducted by the librarians at the Stony Brook campus.[5] The *College Blue Book*[6] and *American Universities and Colleges*[7] were the sources used to select the list of colleges and universities where the questionnaire would be sent.

The questionnaire consisted of eight major questions designed to establish a comparison between the academic faculty and the librarians of the same institutions. The questions were phrased in such a manner as to establish a valid comparison relevant to the above definition of "full faculty status." The following were asked:

1. Is faculty rank given to librarians, or do they have special titles?
2. What are the criteria for promotion: research, seniority, publications, advanced degrees, teaching, or work performance?
3. What is required to achieve tenure; are librarians given the same privileges as teaching faculty?
4. Who at the institution is eligible for sabbatical leave, and at what rank?
5. Is the academic appointment for faculty and librarians based on twelve or

[4]Composed with the assistance of Dr. Howard Clayton, now with the University of Oklahoma.

[5]An informal study on status of the State University of New York librarians conducted by a committee of librarians at State University Center at Stony Brook, July 1967.

[6]*The College Blue Book* (12th ed.; Los Angeles: College Planning Programs, Ltd., 1968).

[7]*American Universities and Colleges* (9th ed.; Washington, D.C.: American Council on Education, 1964).

nine months? Is summer employment optional and separately compensated?
6. Are all academic vacations given to both faculty and librarians?
7. Who participates in the faculty government and who has voting rights and representation?
8. What are the fringe benefits and to whom are they given?

At the end of the questionnaire the librarians' evaluation was solicited regarding the degree of status they had attained in their own institution, and further comments were requested.

The questionnaires were sent to 321 colleges and universities throughout the United States in October 1967. Two hundred returns (62.3 per cent) were received, of which the committee was able to analyze 183, giving a return of 57 per cent. Many replies were received in the form of letters. The questionnaire was subsequently registered with the American Council on Education and assigned No. QR5544.

The last step in the investigation involved the tabulation and interpretation of the results. To make the analysis of data more efficient, a code sheet was set up and the answers transcribed into numerical values. The values were converted into IBM readable data. The data processing division at State University of New York College at Brockport assisted in analysis of the data.

FINDINGS

The statistical analysis shows that only twenty-six of 183, or 14.2 per cent, of the reporting libraries grant "full faculty status" to librarians.[8] The low 14.2 per cent figure was a result of strict adherence to the definition of "full faculty status." To qualify under the definition an institution had to allow its librarians equality in all categories. Twenty-one libraries which showed slight deviations were therefore accounted as not having "full faculty status." These libraries varied in only one of the following areas: librarians were not permitted, expected, or encouraged to engage in research; to teach credit-carrying courses; to take complete academic vacations; or to participate fully in faculty government. If these variations had been allowed, the figure for reporting libraries with faculty

[8]Colorado State University, Fort Collins; Eastern Illinois University, Charleston; Illinois State University, Normal; Fort Hays Kansas State College, Hays; Northwestern State College of Louisiana, Natchitoches; Moorhead State College, Moorhead, Minn.: Winona State College, Winona, Minn.; Southeast Missouri State College, Cape Girardeau; Southwest Missouri State College, Springfield; Glassboro State College, Glassboro, N.J.; Newark State College, Union City, N.J.: Appalachian State University, Boone, N.C.; Northwestern State College, Alva, Okla.; Edinboro State College, Edinboro, Pa.; Millersville State College, Millersville, Pa.; Shippensburg State College, Shippensburg, Pa.; Westchester State College, Westchester, Pa.; Sam Houston State College, Huntsville, Tex.; Texas A. & M. University, College Station; University of Houston, Houston, Tex.; Western Washington State College, Bellingham; Wisconsin State University, Eau Claire; Wisconsin State University, La Crosse; Stout State University, Menomonie, Wis.; Wisconsin State University, Oshkosh; Wisconsin State University, Stevens Point.

status would have been 25.7 per cent. The last question of the questionnaire dealt with the self-evaluation of the respondents as to whether or not they felt they had full faculty status at their particular institution. The answers to this question were very revealing: almost two thirds, or 63.4 per cent, of the reporting librarians consider themselves as having full faculty status, but only 14.2 per cent of the total answering met our criteria of "full faculty status." The high percentage of librarians reporting that they had full faculty status might be attributed to the fact that librarians themselves are not aggressive in this area. They do not expect or demand equal treatment from their institutions nor do they see themselves in the same professional light as the rest of the academic faculty.

Table 1
REGIONAL DISTRIBUTION OF FULL ACADEMIC STATUS OF
LIBRARIANS IN STATE UNIVERSITIES AND FOUR—YEAR COLLEGES

Region	Total No. Reporting	With Complete Academic Status No.	Per Cent
New England	17	0	0.0
Middle Atlantic*	30*	6*	20*
Southern States	36	3	8.3
Midwestern States	58	12	20.7
Rocky Mountains	10	1	10.0
Southwestern States	23	3	13.0
Pacific Coast States	21	1	4.8
Alaska	1	0	0.0
Hawaii	1	0	0.0
Total	197*	26	13.1

*Including fourteen State University of New York colleges and university centers which were not questioned for this survey since data were obtained prior to the sending of the questionnaire.

To establish table 1 the total responses were sorted by regions to ascertain if any pattern of distribution could be detected. In order not to distort the regional results, information was included on State University of New York university centers and four-year colleges which had been obtained by questionnaire prior to this particular study.

As shown in figure 1 a regional fluctuation did emerge. The midwestern region, represented by the largest number of responses, fifty-eight, had also the highest percentage, 20.7 per cent, of institutions with "full faculty status." The midwestern region consisted of Michigan, Ohio, Wisconsin, Indiana, Illinois, Minnesota, Nebraska, Iowa, Missouri, North and South Dakota, and Kansas. Next followed the middle Atlantic states with 20 per cent. Six regions had representa-

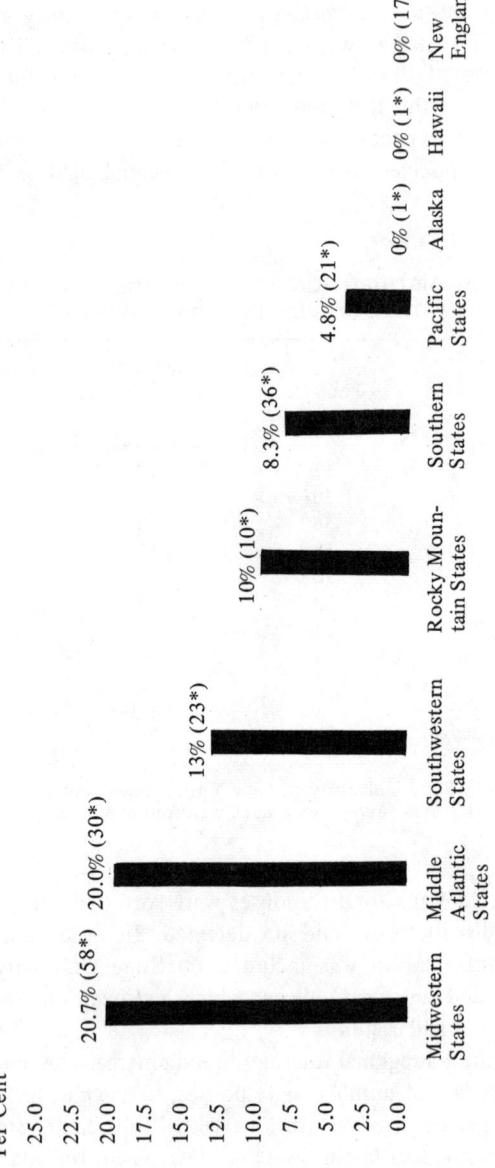

*Number of institutions reporting.

Fig. 1. Pattern of regional distribution: per cent with complete academic status

tion among the librarians with "full faculty status," while three regions, New England, Alaska, and Hawaii reported no institutions that could fulfill the established criteria. Surprisingly, there was not a single institution in the New England area reporting "full faculty status." As one librarian from New England reported, "I have had just one fully qualified person on my staff in the fourteen years I have been here and lost that one to a neighboring university where status is given."

After the tabulation of data for regional distribution was completed, an effort was made to find out if the size of the institution would have any bearing on "full faculty status." The responses were divided into three categories according to the size of the student population. The first group consisted of colleges with four thousand or fewer students, the second of those between 4,001 to 12,000 students, and the third group included all the colleges with 12,001 students and above. Computing all variables, the result was consistent. The middle group of colleges (those having between 4,001 and 12,000 students) had the highest frequency of "full faculty status." Examples of this finding are the state university systems of Pennsylvania, New Jersey, and Missouri, where the large universities do not have full faculty status but the four-year institutions do. The study indicated that middle-sized institutions are ahead of their larger and smaller sister institutions in giving recognition to the library profession.

Table 2
STATISTICAL ANALYSIS OF QUESTIONNAIRE BY MAJOR CRITERIA

	Librarians & Faculty Same Per Cent	Librarians & Faculty Different Per Cent	No Response Per Cent
Academic titles	65.0	29.5	5.5
Promotion policies	49.7	27.9	22.4
Tenure criteria	77.6	15.8	6.6
Sabbatical leave	74.3	20.2	5.5
Rate of pay	29.0	62.8	8.2
Academic vacations	33.9	62.3	3.8
Faculty government	71.0	17.5	11.5
Fringe benefits	89.6	4.9	5.5

Table 2 reflects the over-all comparison of librarians to faculty within the framework established by the aforementioned definition of "full faculty status." It should be noted that among the privileges given to librarians, fringe benefits and tenure criteria occur most frequently, with sabbatical leave, faculty government, and academic titles ranking next. Faculty promotion policies, academic vacations, and rate of pay, in that order, are less often available to librarians. The area of least equality was rate of pay, with only 29.0 per cent of respondents being equal. The next lowest area was that of academic vacations, with 33.9 per cent of respondents being equal. It is interesting to note that although 65.0 per cent of librarians have academic titles, such titles do not guarantee equal privileges since only 29.0 per cent have the same rate of pay as the faculty. Almost half of the libraries reporting, 49.7 per cent, indicated that the staff is judged for promotion by the same criteria as faculty, including research and publications. However, only 33.9 per cent of librarians have equal vacations.

It is apparent from table 3 that in 74.9 per cent of the libraries reporting, work performance is most frequently used as a criterion for promotion. To put it differently, an overwhelming three fourths of the libraries reporting still attach significant importance to work performance. Almost two thirds, or 63.4 per cent, of the libraries consider advanced degrees as the second most frequently used factor for evaluation of professional librarians. Seniority, which only a decade ago would have topped the list, interestingly enough ranks third in order of frequency with 43.2 per cent. A glance at the table reveals that only sixty-five, or 35.5 per cent, of the institutions attached some importance to research and publications by librarians, which might be due to the fact that many administrators do not free librarians from their duties to work in independent research projects.

Table 3
CRITERIA USED FOR PROMOTIONS OF ACADEMIC LIBRARIANS IN DESCENDING ORDER OF FREQUENCY

| | | Number of Libraries Reporting | | | | | |
| | | Yes | | No | | No Response | |
Criteria	Total No.	No.	Per Cent	No.	Per Cent	No.	Per Cent
Work Performance	183	137	74.9	14	7.6	32	17.5
Advanced Degrees	183	116	63.4	29	15.8	38	20.8
Seniority	183	79	43.2	64	35.0	40	21.8
Research	183	65	35.5	83	45.4	35	19.1

CONCLUSION

It is unfortunate, but nonetheless true, that the conditions of librarians have not changed significantly over the past decade. Even though 63.4 per cent of librarians polled reported that they had status, findings indicate that they did not. The yardstick by which the committee measured the librarians' faculty status might be considered by some to be too rigid. This is indicated by the repeated responses from our colleagues saying "we are equal to faculty, except . . . ." These statements suggest that librarians themselves may be somewhat responsible for their position on a low rung of the academic ladder. They are willing to settle for less than equal status, and some even seemed resigned to their fate. "We are just rendering a service," one respondent wrote. "We have sacrificed to learn, but feel that except for appreciation from alumni and students, the administration does not know we are here." Another stated, "Librarians have been conned into thinking it is vulgar and unprofessional to care about status and rank."

The institutions of higher education must also bear some of the blame, for they have rightfully insisted upon upgrading libraries and librarians and their qualifications, but many have ignored the pleas of librarians to be treated at par with the rest of the faculty of which they are an integral part. Neither can the academic community be absolved from the responsibility of holding librarians at an unequal and unjust level. Each time the question of equal status for librarians arises, the teaching faculty creates an uproar as if the attainment of status is their sole right and extending the same privileges to others is an infringement of this right.

If librarians are to improve their own situation, they and their professional organizations must work toward gaining their proper place in the academic community. This implies that librarians must accept the fact that "full faculty status" brings with it not only equal privileges but also the obligations of research and advanced degrees which have become synonymous with faculty status. The American Library Association has not taken a strong stand on this issue. This is unlike the action taken by other professional organizations, such as the American Association of University Professors, which has played an active role in ameliorating the conditions of academic faculties. The granting of "full faculty status" by the colleges throughout the nation appears to be one of the imperative actions to be pursued in alleviating the acute shortage of academic librarians.

Principles governing the employment of nonprofessional personnel in university libraries

Robert H. Muller

Dr. Muller is Professor, School of Library Science, and Research Consultant to the University Library, University of Michigan. This article appeared earlier in *College and Research Libraries,* May 1965.

By far the highest proportion of the staff of a university library (in some cases 75 per cent) consists of nonprofessional personnel. The term *nonprofessional* is unfortunate since it fails to convey a clear notion of the important responsibilities carried by nonprofessionals and may imply a lack of recognition or appreciation. It should, therefore, be stressed that a university library could not operate efficiently without such a supporting staff. Duties assigned to nonprofessionals include typing; filing; searching; checking; recording; shelving; labeling; bookkeeping; mending; answering simple information questions at public desks; operating printing, photographic, and other machinery; handling supplies; preparing materials for binding; keeping statistics; collecting fines, etc. The borderline between what is nonprofessional and what is professional among library duties has become more sharply defined in recent years due in part to the shortage of library school graduates and the need to operate libraries as efficiently and economically as possible.

It is recognized as a sound principle of library management that professional librarians should not be employed for the performance of nonprofessional tasks except in emergencies or unusual circumstances. The application of this principle requires that a competent nonprofessional staff of sufficient size be employed and retained by all libraries. If a library is unable to attract competent nonprofessional employees or if the turnover among such employees is excessively high, there is a risk that librarians will be forced into the performance of nonprofessional tasks to an excessive extent and thus provide library service that is economically indefensible and detrimental to the wider public acceptance of librarians as a professional group. Failure to provide adequate and stable nonprofessional staffing to assist the professional library staff also results in a lowering of the attractiveness of librarianship as a career and thus makes recruiting efforts to the profession increasingly difficult.

At institutions where regulations governing nonacademic employees are not under the jurisdiction of or subject to the influence of the library administration, it will of course be necessary to comply with existing regulations. In cases where the library administration is in a position to bring influence to bear upon the conditions governing the employment of the nonprofessional staff of the library, the best possible conditions governing the employment of nonprofessional personnel should be maintained. The following list represents an attempt to enumerate important conditions contributing to a favorable employment situation:

1. Compensation, length of the workweek, and fringe benefits should be the same as those governing nonacademic employment elsewhere on a given campus. In a tight local labor market it is necessary to offer better-than-average salaries and fringe benefits in order to attract the best possible nonprofessional employees to the library and retain them.
2. A personnel classification and pay plan assuring equal pay for equal work should provide a sufficient number of classes to allow for differences in the complexity of work.
3. Merit increases should be provided within grade.
4. Fringe benefits should include group hospitalization insurance, a retirement plan, sick-leave allowance, and a disability plan.
5. Continuing employment should be preceded by a probationary period of reasonable length. Continuing employment, however, would not be as permanent as or on a par with faculty tenure, but would mean that employment would normally be terminated only in case of proven unsatisfactory performance or insufficiency of institutional funds.
6. Minimum vacation allowance should be one day per month. If possible vacation allowance should increase after a specified length of service in order to induce employees to continue their work in the library for as long as possible.

In addition to these basic conditions, and perhaps more important than any one of them, is the goal of giving each employee a genuine sense of identification with the team effort of the library by encouraging him to make suggestions concerning the improvement of procedures and policies and to provide appropriate incentives and rewards for such efforts. Through the furtherance of the sense of self-esteem of the nonprofessional group of the library team and the encouragement of free communication among all members of a library staff, morale can be strengthened and quality of performance improved.

Given such conditions, the nonprofessional staff of a library may be expected to develop a deep sense of loyalty to the employing library, a high degree of service-mindedness, and a respect for the mission of libraries as indispensable social institutions.

Status of college and university librarians

This report was prepared by the Committee on Academic Status of ACRL's University Libraries Section, adopted by the Section during the Washington Conference, and approved for ALA by the ACRL Board of Directors in a post-Conference mail vote. Arthur M. McAnally, Director of Libraries and of the School of Library Science, University of Oklahoma, is chairman of the committee. Other members are Robert B. Downs, Dean of Library Administration, University of Illinois; William H. Jesse, Director of Libraries, University of Tennessee; Archie L. McNeal, Director of Libraries, University of Miami; and Sidney B. Smith, Director of Libraries, Louisiana State University.

The University Libraries Section of ACRL, recognizing the mutual interests of faculty members and librarians in the dissemination of knowledge and the advancement of learning, knowing that the work of professional librarians is essentially educational in character, and convinced that the institution benefits substantially when library activities are integrated with teaching and research plans, strongly recommends that professional librarians be granted academic status, with corresponding faculty privileges.

STATUS ALREADY GRANTED

Over half of the colleges and universities in the country have already recognized the propriety and value of academic status for their professional library staffs by granting academic recognition to professional librarians. Sometimes full faculty status is granted, with academic rank and titles; in other instances librarians are recognized formally as members of the academic family with equivalent and corresponding ranks. Whether academic or full faculty status shall be granted is a matter of individual determination by each institution. However, the essential educational nature of the librarian's duties has been recognized increasingly by administrators, faculties, professional societies, and accrediting agencies. For example, the society of college faculty members, the American Association of University Professors, states that "librarians of professional status are engaged in teaching and research,"[1] and are eligible for membership provided their own institution consents. Some accrediting agencies have stipulated faculty rank for professional library staff.

REASONS TO GRANT ACADEMIC STATUS

Academic recognition for professional librarians seems quite logical for educational reasons. Recent developments in higher education and in librarianship make this recognition desirable and feasible.

1. Demands upon academic libraries have increased greatly during recent years. The ever-quickening tempo of research, with a corresponding upward spiral in rates of publication throughout the world, make effective library service even more important to the maintenance of a high quality of instruction and research. Similarly, the proliferation of subjects, ever-increasing specialization, and the need to handle a variety of foreign languages also raise the level of ability that is required to cope with this great flood of information.

2. Curricular and educational requirements have caused academic libraries to become more responsive. One concrete evidence of this growing responsiveness is the reorganization of many libraries along subject lines since 1938. Other libraries have been reoriented towards student interests by establishing undergraduate or lower division libraries. A great many libraries, recognizing accessibility as a factor in use, have provided educational stimuli by putting more books on open shelves. This reorientation has made the library more flexible and more usable as a teaching instrument; consequently, librarians have undertaken increased teaching, counseling, and research activities. These trends also have placed greater emphasis upon competence in subject areas as well as in the professional aspects of library work.

3. The educational scope of institutions has been broadened through increased offering of public education, institutes, short courses, exhibits, museums, and publication programs. Institutions also have achieved wider audiences for public service through the medium of television. All of these increase the demands for effective library service.

4. The educational qualifications of librarians have been improved, and there has been an improvement in the personality and understanding of people recruited to the library profession. The first professional degree is now at the master's level, due to improvements in library education since 1948.

5. Advances in research, professional writing, and progress in the field also are doing much to establish librarianship as a mature profession.

6. Institutions are demanding librarians of high calibre to meet the growing demands. To attract the most capable personnel, satisfactory status is necessary,

[1]Cited in Robert B. Downs, "The Current Status of University Library Staffs," in R. B. Downs, ed., *The Status of American College and University Librarians* (ACRL Monograph no. 22; Chicago: ALA, 1958), p.25.

for librarians are becoming aware of the importance of status. Librarians now have a choice of positions due to a shortage of librarians that has existed since World War II. It is safe to say that any institution not granting academic status to its professional librarians will find it increasingly difficult to recruit a high type of library personnel.

7. Finally, librarians need the protection of academic freedom to build broad and varied collections unrestricted by prejudice, bigotry, or special pressures.

DEFINITION

Academic status for professional librarians may be defined as the formal recognition, in writing, by an institution's authorities, of librarians as members of the instructional and research staff. The recognition may take the form of assigned faculty ranks and titles, or equivalent ranks and titles, according to institutional custom.

OBLIGATIONS OF ACADEMIC STATUS

Status carries with it certain definite responsibilities for the individual. These correspond to the librarian's obligations to his profession, to support it and contribute to its advancement. The first requirement is for intellectual activity, including a keen interest in the intellectual life of the campus. The librarian must accept responsibility for independent learning and continual intellectual growth. Next, the librarian must accept responsibility for educational statesmanship; his activity touches upon all areas of academic life. Status also calls for the highest level of professionalism in performance of his duties.

The librarian must be a creative member of the academic community. He performs an educational function and should be interested in research and publication to advance the frontiers of his profession, or in administrative studies which make a contribution to this advancement. He should be interested in professional organizations, and has an obligation for faithful service to his institution.

The director of a library has the responsibility of furthering the professional advancement of the staff. He must facilitate their professional advancement, encourage educational progress, formal or informal, in professional and in other subject areas; provide for a careful separation of professional and nonprofessional activities, to the end that professional librarians are enabled to use their abilities to the fullest; scrupulously adhere to the highest standards in appointments and promotions; recognize that promotion in rank does not necessarily require the performance of administrative duties; and through democracy in administration utilize the abilities of the professional staff in the management of the library.

Only a portion of the work that must be performed in a library requires professional training and ability. Routine and nonprofessional tasks are performed by clerical and subprofessional staff. It must be understood clearly that academic status is recommended only for professional librarians, who need and are entitled to it.

PRIVILEGES OF ACADEMIC STATUS

Along with the contributions which library staff members make because of academic status, there are certain privileges which they in turn may expect. These relate to tenure, academic freedom, sabbatical leaves, equitable salaries, holidays, insurance, and retirement.

ACRL urges all academic institutions to recognize the similarity of education, training, and goals of faculty members and librarians, and to formalize that similarity so that the cause of education can be beneficially and creatively improved by bringing into close harmony the requirements and obligations, as well as the privileges, which faculty and library staff should share in the great work of improving American education.

Status of academic librarians in retrospect

Robert B. Downs

Dr. Downs is Dean of Library Administration, University of Illinois. His article here is reprinted from *College and Research Libraries,* July 1968.

The idea of the college and university librarian as a bona fide member of the academic community has matured slowly, and rearguard actions against it continue to our own day. How far the profession has progressed over the past one hundred years may be judged by a brief historical review.

Examination of a cross section of the annual catalogs or registers of United States universities, private and public, for 1870-71 reveals something of the status of librarians in leading institutions nearly a century ago.

Columbia College (later Columbia University) lists the librarian, assistant librarian, and school of mines librarian under "Officers of Instruction and Government," without academic titles. California at Berkeley included William Swinton as librarian and Professor of English, under "Faculty and Officers." Cornell University placed Professor Willard Fiske as "Librarian" under a special heading after "Faculty of the University." Dartmouth College, however, recorded the librarian's name with "Faculty," though without rank. Harvard's solution was to list the librarian and assistant librarian under "Officers of Instruction and Government." The University of Illinois used a curious title: "Librarian and Assistant Teacher." Indiana University lumped the librarian under "College Officers." At Iowa State University, the librarian doubled as Professor of Latin. The University of Michigan included the librarian and assistant librarian under the heading of "Members of Faculties and Other Officers." There was a remarkable situation at the University of Minnesota, where William W. Folwell held the combined position of president and librarian. Neither Northwestern University, nor the University of Pennsylvania, nor the University of Wisconsin was sufficiently aware of the librarian's existence to mention him in its catalog. At Princeton, the librarian was Professor of Greek, and the assistant librarian was Tutor in Greek. Yale listed the librarian, assistant librarian, and registrar at the end of the section entitled "Faculty, Instructors, and Officers."

As of 1870-71, according to this representative sample, none of the universities gave their chief librarians academic titles, unless they were members of the teaching faculty. Apparently there was a feeling in some institutions that the head librarians ought to be grouped with the faculty, but what the relationship should be was undetermined. Consequently, the usual practice was to list them after the regular teaching staff, with their professional titles, together with registrars, museum curators, and other miscellaneous officers.

In extenuation of the institutions for their uncertainty about the place of librarians in the academic scene, it should be noted that a century ago American college libraries were in their infancy. When the American Library Association was organized in 1876, only two college libraries in the country contained more than fifty thousand volumes each, Harvard alone possessing more than one hundred thousand volumes. Library staffs were minuscule in size, in part because of the minuteness of the libraries and in part because demands on them were limited. Few faculty members held doctorates or carried on research, and students had little occasion to use the library collections.

In the famous 1876 United States Bureau of Education special report, *Public Libraries in the United States of America,*[1] F. B. Perkins and William Mathews proposed the creation of "professorships of books and reading," to guide students through the mazes of what even then was regarded as a bibliographical explosion. The instruction recommended would be primarily for the acquisition of knowledge, "the scientific use of books," *i.e.,* sound methodology, and for "literary production." A chair of books and reading, it was suggested, might be filled by "an accomplished librarian." The first library school was still eleven years away.

By the beginning of the present century, modest advances in the status of librarians were evident. In no instance, however, among eighteen major universities checked did the librarian hold an academic title as librarian *per se.* The situation was as follows:

Brown University listed the librarian, assistant librarian, and four library staff members with "Officers of Administration and Instruction." California at Berkeley included the librarian in the Academic Senate, but without academic rank; the remainder of the library staff was lumped under "Assistants and Other Officers." The University of Chicago recognized the librarian by making him a member of the University Senate and University Council. At Columbia

---

[1]U.S. Bureau of Education, *Public Libraries in the United States of America; Their History, Condition, and Management, Special Report* (Washington: Government Printing Office, 1876), p.230-51.

the librarian was among "Officers of Administration"; other staff members were listed at the head of a brief sketch of the library. Cornell listed the librarian and his staff as a group under "Officers of Instruction and Administration." Harvard did the same. At Illinois the librarian was a member of the Senate and Council and a professor, but by virtue of being director also of the library school; other librarians were listed with "Laboratory and Other Assistants." Indiana used the heading of "Library Officers" following the listing of "Faculty."

Iowa placed the librarian with "Administrative Officers" and also listed the librarian and his staff as a group under "Members of the Faculties," between lecturers and instructors. Under "Members of the Faculties and Other Officers," Michigan placed the librarian with full professors, though without rank. At Missouri the librarian was one of "Other Officers." North Carolina included him among "Officers of Administration" and listed two other staff members under a sketch on the "University Library." Northwestern's heading of "Officers of Instruction and Government" included the librarian, and Pennsylvania named its librarian and assistant librarian under "Administrative Officers." Like Michigan, Princeton listed the librarian with full professors, but without an academic title; the associate librarian and reference librarian were in the list of assistant professors, again minus formal rank. A similar plan was followed by Stanford, where the librarian and associate librarian were grouped with associate professors, the assistant librarian with instructors, and other staff members with assistants. Both Texas and Wisconsin grouped the librarians and their staffs together following the listing of faculty and other officers. Finally, at Yale the librarian and assistant librarian were under the heading of "Faculty and Instructors," again without titles; the rest of the library staff were with "Other Officers" at the end of the faculty list.

A definite trend is observable in the 1900-1901 sample in the direction of rating the head librarians as faculty, despite the fact that no breakthrough had been made toward conferring formal academic titles on them. Other than the chief librarians and one or two top associates, however, it is obvious that professional library staff members lacked any definite place in the educational hierarchy.

Voices crying in the wilderness were trying to make themselves heard at an early date. H. A. Sawtelle, writing on college librarianship, is quoted in the *Library Journal,* June 1878, as follows:

Time was when if a college librarian cataloged and placed his books and for half an hour twice a week charged the borrowed volumes and checked the return ones, he had sufficiently discharged his duty. But it has come to be understood that it becomes him to be daily ready to be consulted in relation to any book or subject, to converse freely with the students in regard to their reading, inspiring their literary interest, guiding their taste, bringing to their attention the right kind of appetizing works, and if needful gently leading on the reader from light and tasty books to those of high quality and permanent utility. To us nothing in the life of the college student seems to be of greater importance than just this inspiration and guidance. But all this is time consuming and requires no small amount of understanding and skill.

The writer concluded that such college librarianship as he described "ought not to be annexed to a professorship, but be itself a professorship."[2]

As early as 1891, President Gilman of Johns Hopkins University made the statement that: "The librarian's office should rank with that of professor. . . . The profession of librarian should be distinctly recognized. Men and women should be encouraged to enter it, should be trained to discharge its duties, and should be regarded, promoted, and honored in proportion to the services they render."[3]

Enlightened librarians realized that they ought to have more clearly defined status, as is revealed by stirrings in the profession early in the current century. For example, W. E. Henry, librarian of the University of Washington, speaking at the ALA conference in Pasadena in 1911, after defending the training and scholarly nature of the work of college librarians, asserted:

With such preparation and such relationship to the educational processes I shall claim that the library staff must rank with the faculty or teaching staff of any department. The librarian or head of the staff should have the rank and pay of a professor; the assistant librarian . . . should be accorded the rank and pay of an associate professor; and the other members of the staff that of assistant professor or instructor, this to be determined by the nature of the work, the preparation and particular ability required; and those not fitted to so rank should not be members of the staff but some other name should be adopted.[4]

Mr. Henry's goal had not been achieved at the University of Washington at the time of his address. The librarian and five members of his staff were grouped under "Library Staff," without academic titles, near the end of the section on "Faculty and Officers." According to returns from questionnaires sent by Henry to sixteen college and university libraries across the country, however, he reported, "it appears that the librarian usually has the rank of a professor [sans title?] Below the librarian all sorts of conditions prevail."[5]

[2]H. A. Sawtelle, "The College Librarianship," *Library Journal*, III (June 1878), 162.

[3]D. C. Gilman, "University Libraries, an Address at the Opening of the Sage Library of Cornell University, October 7, 1891," *University Problems in the United States* (1898), p.245-55.

[4]W. E. Henry, "The Academic Standing of College Library Assistants and Their Relation to the Carnegie Foundation," *Bulletin of the American Library Association*, V (May 1911), 259-60.

[5]*Ibid.*, 262.

An important step forward was taken in the same year, 1911, by the Columbia University trustees, who ruled: "The librarian shall have the rank of professor, the assistant librarian that of associate professor and the supervisors shall rank as assistant professors and bibliographers as instructors." From Harvard University it was reported that "librarians and assistant librarians" were eligible to participate in the faculty retirement system.

A few years later E. C. Richardson, noted librarian of Princeton University, reviewed the place of the library in a university and concluded that its position would be determined by the effectiveness with which its teaching function was discharged. Richardson pointed out that the growth of research work, the advent of the research professor, and the establishment of library schools had brought librarians "into the circle of the teaching faculties."[6] Authoritative support for this contention came from President Nicholas Murray Butler of Columbia, who held that the library was coordinate with the various professional schools and main departments of the university, the librarian ranking as a. dean, and various members of the professional staff standing in parallel order with professors, assistant professors, and instructors of the other faculties.[7]

About the same time a strong statement from W. N. C. Carlton, librarian, Newberry Library, objected to the fact that in some institutions "the librarian is not granted a seat and vote in the faculty. This," the writer went on, "is a viciously bad practice. Its evils are too patent to need illustration. If a man is not qualified for the duty and responsibility of sharing in the debates, consideration, and decisions relating to general university policy and administration, he ought not to be appointed librarian, whatever his technical qualifications may be."[8]

A subordinate staff member was heard from nearly fifty years ago when J. T. Jennings, then reference librarian of Iowa State College, wrote about "Librarianship as a Profession in College and University Libraries." Jennings was convinced that the chief librarian's position in most college and university communities had become well established "in dignity, in importance, in salary," ranking as the head of one of the most important departments. "But what about the remainder of the library staff?" he asked. "With the exception of a possible assistant librarian they are usually considered 'mere clerks,' as is shown by their salaries, their hours of work, and the attitude of their superiors toward granting them opportunities for advancement." Jennings was inclined to blame this state of affairs on the head librarians who were not sufficiently energetic in encouraging and assisting junior staff members to improve their educational

---

[6] E. C. Richardson, "The Place of the Library in a University," *Ibid.,* X (January 1916), 1-13.

[7] *Ibid.,* V (1911), 13.

[8] W. N. C. Carlton, "Universities and Librarians," *Public Libraries,* XX (December 1915), 455.

and professional preparation, as junior members of the teaching faculty were expected to do.[9]

The same conclusion was reached by another reference librarian, Edith M. Coulter, of the University of California, writing in 1917. Even the chief librarians, she pointed out, lacked certain privileges customarily belonging to the teaching faculty, such as extended vacations, leaves of absence, and sabbaticals for advanced study and research. Proper recognition would come to librarians, Miss Coulter held, if they participated more actively in teaching *e.g.,* bibliographic instruction to university students; if the programs of library schools were standardized, more doctoral degrees were held by librarians, requirements for appointments to university library staffs were raised, professional and clerical duties were differentiated, and more study and research were done by librarians. Miss Coulter displayed remarkable foresight in urging a doctoral program in library science more than a decade before the establishment of the graduate library school in Chicago.[10]

The first full exploration of the status of professional librarians was undertaken by George A. Works, in his *College and University Library Problems,* based on data collected in 1925. In a chapter devoted to the subject, Dr. Works reviewed types of library work, factors affecting the status of a library staff, current conditions, the relative preparation of library and teaching staffs, comparative salaries, work schedules, and retirement provisions. Among the important conclusions were these: (1) insufficient distinction is made in libraries between clerical and professional types of service, but there are a number of positions in every large library whose requirements in professional education and experience are comparable with the requirements for positions in the various grades in the teaching staff; (2) among the seventeen institutions studied, wide differences were found, varying from those in which librarians held faculty rank to others in which the library staff, except the librarian and perhaps one or two others, were classified as clerical; (3) in some universities, *e.g.,* Columbia and Stanford, librarians were given equivalent status, but not considered members of the instructional staff; (4) except for the head librarian, salaries of the library staff were generally lower than those of comparable members of the faculty; (5) the academic preparation of faculty members of all professional ranks was more advanced than that of library department heads; (6) no account was taken of the fact that annual periods of service were ordinarily longer for members of the library staff than for the teaching staff; (7) retirement provisions varied: seven institutions had no allowance for faculty or librarians; six had the same

[9]J. T. Jennings, "Librarianship as a Profession in College and University Libraries," *Library Journal,* XLIII (April 1918), 227-33.

[10]Edith M. Coulter, "The University Librarian: His Preparation, Position and Relation to the Academic Department of the University," *Bulletin of the American Library Association,* XVI (July 1922), 271-75.

retirement arrangements for both groups, and three had different arrangements for faculty and librarians.[11]

A decade later an outstanding university president, Henry M. Wriston, whose ideas have had considerable impact on academic library service, set forth his concept of the proper relationships between the college librarian and the teaching staff. "The librarian," concluded Dr. Wriston, "despite his administrative duties is primarily an officer of instruction. He should have the scholarly interests and tastes which are expected of other members of the faculty. He should be given faculty status and should participate in all the committee and other discussions incidental to that status." In harmony with this proposal, the writer added that the library "should be treated not as an ancillary enterprise but as one of the central sources of motive power for the operation of the institution."[12]

During the past thirty years the literature relating to the status of college and university librarians has proliferated, including the findings of a number of comprehensive surveys. The first, after Works, was Miriam C. Maloy's study, published in 1939. Among the 129 institutions investigated, Mrs. Maloy found that ninety-eight chief librarians had faculty status, and thirty-one did not; among assistant and associate librarians, thirty had faculty status and forty did not; department heads had faculty status in twenty-seven libraries and no academic rank in four; and professional assistants were granted faculty status in twenty libraries, but not in thirty others. In each of the four categories, the status frequently was nominal.[13]

Following shortly after the Maloy study were a number of other general or limited investigations: James A. McMillen examined the status of library staff members of large universities (1940);[14] Robert W. McEwen, the status of college librarians (1941);[15] Rice Estes, faculty status in the City College Libraries (1941);[16] general surveys were reported by Leonard H. Kirkpatrick (1947),[17] Morris A. Gelfand (1948),[18] Humphrey G. Bousfield (1948),[19] and by Frank

[11]George A. Works, "The Status of the Professional Staff," in his *College and University Library Problems,* (Chicago: ALA, 1927), p.80-98.

[12]Henry M. Wriston, "The College Librarian and the Teaching Staff," *Bulletin of the American Library Association,* XXIX (April 1935), 182.

[13]Miriam C. Maloy, "Faculty Status of College Librarians," *ALA Bulletin,* XXXIII (April 1939), 232-33, 302.

[14]James A. McMillen, "Academic Status of Library Staff Members of Large Universities," *College and Research Libraries,* I (March 1940), 138-40.

[15]Robert W. McEwen, "The Status of College Librarians," *Ibid.,* III (June 1942), 256-61.

[16]Rice Estes, "Faculty Status in the City College Libraries," *Ibid.,* III (December 1941), 43-45.

[17]Leonard H. Kirkpatrick, "Another Approach to Staff Status," *Ibid.,* VIII (July 1947), 218-20.

[18]Morris A. Gelfand, "The College Librarian in the Academic Community," *Ibid.,* X (April 1949), 129-34, 139.

[19]Humphrey G. Bousfield, "College Libraries with Dual Roles," *Ibid.,* IX (January 1948), 25-32.

A. Lundy (1951)[20] and Lawrence S. Thompson (1952)[21] as well as by Robert
B. Downs (1954 and 1957);[22] and Robert H. Muller reviewed the question of
faculty rank for library staff members in medium-sized universities and colleges
(1953).[23] Evidence of lively continued interest is shown by more recent articles
published by Carlson,[24] Knapp,[25] Branscomb,[26] McAnally,[27] Veit,[28] and
others.

Progress achieved by university librarians since the first feeble beginnings a
century ago may be estimated further from a summary of conditions prevailing
in 1964.[29] Academic status for librarians, it was then reported, had become
firmly established in a considerable number of American universities. New con-
verts, principally among state institutions, had swelled the ranks of those universities where librarians are accorded the responsibilities and perquisites of academic or faculty status. Considerable diversity was discovered, however, among
the forms of recognition received. In certain instances, agreement upon the
principle of academic standing for librarians was limited or qualified. The
struggle by academic librarians for improved standing obviously continues,
but with increasing prospects for general acceptance.

[20]Frank A. Lundy, "Faculty Rank for Professional Librarians," *Ibid.* XII (January 1951),
11-19, 109-22.

[21]Lawrence S. Thompson, "Preparation and Status of Personnel," *Library Trends,* I
(July 1952), 95-104.

[22]Robert B. Downs, "Are College and University Librarians Academic?" *College and
Research Libraries,* XV (January 1954), 9-14; and "The Current Status of University
Library Staffs," *Ibid.,* XVIII (September 1957), 375-85.

[23]Robert H. Muller, "Faculty Rank for Library Staff Members in Medium-Sized
Universities and Colleges," *Bulletin of the American Association of University Professors,*
XXXIX (Autumn 1953), 421-31.

[24]William H. Carlson, "The Trend Toward Academic Recognition of College Librarians,"
College and Research Libraries, XVI (January 1955), 24-29.

[25]Patricia B. Knapp, "The College Librarian; Sociology of a Professional Specialization,"
Ibid., XVI (January 1955), 66-72.

[26]Lewis C. Branscomb, "The Quest for Faculty Rank," in R. B. Downs, ed. *The Status of
American College and University Librarians* (Chicago: ALA, 1958), p.42-46.

[27]Arthur M. McAnally, "The Dynamics of Securing Academic Status," *College and Re-
search Libraries,* XVIII (September 1957), 386-95; and "Privileges and Obligations of
Academic Status," Lewis C. Branscomb, ed., *The Case for Faculty Status for College and
University Librarians* (Chicago: ALA, 1970), p.1-8.

[28]Fritz Veit, "The Status of the Librarian According to Accrediting Standards of Regional
and Professional Associations," *College and Research Libraries,* XXI (March 1960), 127-35.

[29]Robert B. Downs, "Status of University Librarians–1964," *Ibid.,* XXV (July 1964),
253-58;

Index